High-Impact Tutoring in Math and ELA

High-impact tutoring programs are ramping up across the country to address learning recovery post-COVID. But how do you make the most of them? This invaluable book has the answers!

You'll find out the best ways to implement high-dosage tutoring, including what it is and what it is not, how to overcome common challenges, how to establish a program and create a collaborative team, the role of the tutor, relationship building, onboarding and professional development, high-quality curriculum and study skills, assessing students' needs, incorporating MTSS, and more. In addition, the appendix offers a variety of diagnostic and progress-monitoring tools you can use in your own setting.

With this indispensable resource, you'll have the tools you need to help close the achievement gap so your students can thrive in math and ELA.

Dr. Nicki Newton has been an educator for over 35 years, working both nationally and internationally with students of all ages. She has worked on developing Math Workshop and Guided Math Institutes around the country; visit her website at www.drnickinewton.com. She is also an avid blogger (www.guidedmath.wordpress.com), tweeter (@drnickimath), and pinner (www.pinterest.com/drnicki7).

Dr. Terri Ruyter has worked in schools for close to 40 years as an elementary school classroom teacher, a professor of education, and a district literacy specialist. Most recently, she served as the founding principal of a public pre-K-to-8 school in New York City.

TJ Jemison is a math consultant who specializes in special education, math intervention, and math fact fluency for grades K–5.

Also Available from Dr. Nicki Newton
(www.routledge.com/eyeoneducation)

Day-by-Day Math Thinking Routines in Third Grade:
40 Weeks of Quick Prompts and Activities

Day-by-Day Math Thinking Routines in Fourth Grade:
40 Weeks of Quick Prompts and Activities

Day-by-Day Math Thinking Routines in Fifth Grade:
40 Weeks of Quick Prompts and Activities

Leveling Math Workstations in Grades K–2:
Strategies for Differentiated Practice

Daily Math Thinking Routines in Action:
Distributed Practices Across the Year

Mathematizing Your School:
Creating a Culture for Math Success
Co-authored by Janet Nuzzie

Math Problem Solving in Action:
Getting Students to Love Word Problems, Grades K–2

Math Problem Solving in Action:
Getting Students to Love Word Problems, Grades 3–5

Math Workshop in Action:
Strategies for Grades K–5

Math Running Records in Action:
A Framework for Assessing Basic Fact Fluency in Grades K–5

Math Workstations in Action:
Powerful Possibilities for Engaged Learning in Grades 3–5

High-Impact Tutoring in Math and ELA

{ AN EVIDENCE-BASED APPROACH TO HELP ALL STUDENTS SUCCEED }

Dr. Nicki Newton and Dr. Terri Ruyter with TJ Jemison

Routledge
Taylor & Francis Group

NEW YORK AND LONDON

Designed cover image: © Getty Images

First published 2026
by Routledge
605 Third Avenue, New York, NY 10158

and by Routledge
4 Park Square, Milton Park, Abingdon, Oxon, OX14 4RN

Routledge is an imprint of the Taylor & Francis Group, an informa business

© 2026 Nicki Newton

The right of Nicki Newton to be identified as author of this work has been asserted in accordance with sections 77 and 78 of the Copyright, Designs and Patents Act 1988.

All rights reserved. No part of this book may be reprinted or reproduced or utilised in any form or by any electronic, mechanical, or other means, now known or hereafter invented, including photocopying and recording, or in any information storage or retrieval system, without permission in writing from the publishers.

Trademark notice: Product or corporate names may be trademarks or registered trademarks, and are used only for identification and explanation without intent to infringe.

ISBN: 978-1-032-40387-8 (hbk)
ISBN: 978-1-032-36542-8 (pbk)
ISBN: 978-1-003-35284-6 (ebk)

DOI: 10.4324/9781003352846

Typeset in Janson
by Apex CoVantage, LLC

To Mom and Pops, Always
Dr. Nicki

To all the school people who work every day to make school a better experience for the children.

And, of course, to the children, for keeping us on our toes, learning every day, and giving us joy.
Terri

To the dedicated educators who show up every day and make a lasting impact on students' lives—your work matters deeply.
TJ

Contents

Acknowledgments		xi
About the Authors		xiii
Foreword		xvii
Prologue		xxi
Chapter 1	The Power of High-Impact Tutoring	1
Chapter 2	Getting Started: It's All About the Team	9
Chapter 3	Tutors	19
Chapter 4	Professional Development	29
Chapter 5	Assessing Assets, Needs, and Next Moves	37
Chapter 6	High-Quality Curriculum	51
Chapter 7	The Math Tutoring Session	65
Chapter 8	The ELA Tutoring Session	73
Chapter 9	Relationships and Social-Emotional Support	79
Chapter 10	Study Skills—"Academic Enablers"	89
Chapter 11	Fostering Collaborative Connections	101
Chapter 12	High-Impact Tutoring and Multitiered Systems of Support	111
Epilogue		121
References		125

Appendix 1	Invitation-to-Participate Letter	137
Appendix 2	School Assessment Plan	139
Appendix 3	High-Impact Tutoring Program Rubric	143
Appendix 4	Observation and Feedback Template	146

Acknowledgments

I would like to thank my family for all of their encouragement and support. I would like to thank my team for helping me stay organized and encouraging me in the work I do. I would like to thank Terri for coming along on the journey and helping me write a deeper, richer book than I could have done on my own. I would like to thank TJ for contributing his knowledge and insight about MTSS. I would like to thank Lauren because she is the best editor ever, and this is somewhere around book 20-plus for us. I would like to thank all of the Routledge staff for helping the book come together including the copywriters, copyeditors, typesetters, and others. I would like to thank all of the districts and schools that I work with throughout the year. It is an honor and a pleasure to work with you. I learn so much every day. This journey of writing a book about high-impact tutoring has been informative. I have learned so much about teachers, tutors, and students. I really believe in the idea of high-impact tutoring, and I think it offers grand possibilities. I hope this book helps educators along the journey.

Dr. Nicki Newton

Like everything in schools, high-impact tutoring can't be done alone. When we adults team together to pose critical questions, identify our own spaces of unfinished learning, and set learning goals and plans for ourselves and our students, our work is more impactful and meaningful. I want to thank Dr. Nicki for being such a good friend and professional thought partner. Dinner-table conversation invariably centers on education and working toward a more just and equitable world. Thank you for inviting me to join you in writing this book in particular and in solving problems of practice in general. Thank you for centering all your work and my learning on theory and the science of learning and teaching. I also want to thank all my colleagues who have pushed my thinking and learning throughout my journey in elementary and middle schools. Our work together has challenged my thinking and deepened my knowledge about how humans learn to read and write and do math.

Dr. Terri Ruyter

I am deeply grateful to my husband, family, and friends for their unwavering support and encouragement—your belief in me fuels my passion and purpose. I also want to acknowledge the incredible collaboration and community I have found within the math education world. To all who have shared ideas, conversations, and inspiration, thank you. Most importantly, my heartfelt appreciation goes to Dr. Nicki for her steadfast support and mentorship. Your guidance and encouragement mean the world to me. I am also thankful for all the educators who are putting in the hard work every day to meet the needs of our students and cultivating young mathematicians.

TJ Jemison

About the Authors

Dr. Nicki Newton
Dr. Nicki Newton is an education consultant who works with schools and districts around the country and Canada on the K–8 math curriculum. She has taught elementary school, middle school, and graduate school. Dr. Nicki has an Ed.M. and an Ed.D. from Teachers College, Columbia University. She is greatly interested in teaching and learning practices around the world and has researched education in Denmark, Guatemala, and India.

Dr. Newton has written more than 40 books on math education. Her ideas and methodologies are implemented around the world. Dr. Newton wrote the game-changing book *Math Running Records*, which has been adopted by school districts around the world to assess and guide instruction of basic math facts. She has also done extensive work on Math Workshop. She has written several books focusing on Math Workshop in general and Guided Math in particular. Dr. Newton wrote a groundbreaking book on Guided Math 12 years ago that is used as the basis for programs around the country. She followed that up with a grade-level series of books on Guided Math to address the needs of specific grade levels. She also has written two books specifically on Math Workshop. Heinemann just published her latest book, *A Teacher's Guide To Math Workshop* (2023), which she co-wrote with Dr. Alison Mello and Janet Nuzzie. Dr. Newton has also been doing a great deal of work around *Accelerating Math Instruction for Learning Recovery*. Teachers College Press, Columbia University just published that book (2023), which is helping to lead the conversation around teaching all students on grade level in math. She is very excited to have completed writing and researching this book about *High-Impact Tutoring in Math and ELA* (2026). She is also currently writing a book entitled *Math Workshop Plus*, which focuses on the intersections of Math Workshop, social-emotional learning, and Universal Design for Learning, with Dr. Mello. She enjoys visiting schools and working with administrators, teachers, and students in their classrooms face-to-face and virtually. Dr. Newton is also currently a part of the curriculum team and one of the writers for the new McGraw Hill Reveal Math series.

Dr. Terri Ruyter

Terri has worked in schools for close to 40 years as an elementary school classroom teacher, a professor of education, and a district literacy specialist. Most recently, she served as the founding principal of a public pre-K-to-8 school in New York City, where she was tasked with establishing a school culture that centered children and supporting them on their individual learning paths, valued the professional expertise of her staff, and respected parents' voices. She has her master's and doctoral degrees from Teachers College, Columbia University.

Terri believes that the best schools keep children at the center of decision-making. That means that all adults involved in the school need to be informed about child development, be careful and close "kid watchers," and acknowledge the social, emotional, and academic skills and ideas that young people bring to the school community. Using an asset-based lens, we can design and facilitate learning experiences that challenge and engage all students and create an environment that provides the space children need to grow and excel.

TJ Jemison

TJ Jemison is a passionate math educator, consultant, and workshop presenter with nearly 30 years of experience in schools. Originally from Vermont, he has dedicated his career to transforming math instruction, working with schools and districts to create engaging, effective learning experiences. With a rich background as a special educator, curriculum developer, and math coach, TJ has taught math to students of all ages, from pre-K through grade 8.

As a sought-after speaker, he leads professional development sessions and provides ongoing coaching across the United States and internationally. He is also the co-author of *Math by the Book*, a resource that connects mathematics and children's literature. Now based in South Florida, TJ enjoys the sunshine while continuing his mission to inspire educators and students alike.

Foreword

In the evolving landscape of today's education, high-impact tutoring emerged as a transformative approach. The concept is elegantly simple: provide consistent, personalized, and intentional academic support to students who need it most. High-impact tutoring offers a pathway to bridge learning gaps and enhance academic confidence as students gain access to grade-level content. This book serves as both a guide and an inspiration for educators to uncover the profound impact and shape the future of equitable learning for all students.

As educators, we are acutely aware of the growing challenges faced by students—whether due to systemic inequities, the aftermath of interrupted learning, or individual barriers that make academic success difficult to achieve. High-impact tutoring does more than address these challenges; it reframes them as opportunities for meaningful intervention. Research has shown that when students receive regular, focused instruction in small groups or one-on-one, the results are not only measurable but life-changing.

But high-impact tutoring is more than a set of instructional practices. It is a mindset rooted in the belief that every student enters our classrooms with assets and knowledge and, with the right support, can thrive. It challenges the status quo, urging educators to reimagine classroom instruction and the learning process. This approach requires intentionality—from building relationships to gaining expertise for tutors to integrating a tutoring system into the broader educational ecosystem.

At the heart of high-impact tutoring lie relationships. The connection between tutor and student must foster trust, which is essential for meaningful learning to happen. When students feel seen, heard, and valued, they are more likely to engage and take risks in their learning. By prioritizing relationships, high-impact tutoring ensures that education is not just transactional but rather a safe environment in which students can build confidence and resilience.

Consistency and the expertise of a well-trained tutor are also pivotal to the success of the tutoring system. A skilled tutor who provides regular, structured sessions that include immediate feedback helps establish routines that reinforce learning as well as build trust. Coupled with ongoing assessments of student needs, this approach ensures that teaching is not only intentional but also responsive.

This book emerges at a critical moment. In the wake of unprecedented disruptions to learning globally, the need for innovative, evidence-based strategies has never been greater. High-impact tutoring has proven to be a lifeline for many students, but its implementation at scale requires thoughtful planning, resource allocation, and unwavering commitment.

In the pages ahead, you will find not only the theoretical underpinnings of high-impact tutoring but also practical insights from those who have successfully implemented it. Through the California Collaborative for Learning Acceleration (CCLA), a statewide initiative focusing on high-impact tutoring as the key evidence-based strategy to accelerate learning, our team has worked with Nicki Newton on numerous occasions. And what I admire about Dr. Nicki's approach is that she feels compelled to experience it as an educator before she writes a book so each piece of the puzzle can work for all students.

As you delve into this text, I encourage you to think of high-impact tutoring not merely as a tool but as a call to action. It is a reminder that education is, at its core, a deeply human endeavor—one that thrives on connection and the belief in every learner's potential. The strategies outlined here are not just about improving test scores; they are about changing lives.

Let this book be your guide as you embark on the journey to make high-impact tutoring a cornerstone of your educational practice. The road might not always be easy, but the rewards are immeasurable.

Happy reading!

Barb Flores
California Collaborative for Learning Acceleration
Santa Clara County Office of Education

Prologue

Relationships Matter . . .

In 2024, I decided to do a cycle of remote tutoring for two grades, third and sixth, in a school I was working in. Little did I realize the lessons I would learn as I ventured off on this journey. The school put a paraprofessional in the room to guide the work. There were three students in each group. Each session lasted 20 minutes. I did two hours, one hour with each grade. I tutored nine students from each grade.

One of those students, Julio, was quite the handful. Julio did a lot of different things that were not in the lesson plans. Julio was a sixth grader who struggled with academics. Julio chose to make laser rods out of the markers instead of actively participating in the lesson. You know how they say that "He got on my nerves." Well, Julio actually laid down on my nerves and did advanced yoga moves. I even kicked Julio out of intervention tutoring for a few days until I realized that I don't do that ever. Then he refused to come, which made me even madder. I started a journal because Julio was taking me through some changes.

I'll let you read it, because this is the stuff that really happens in intervention groups.

What About Julio?

Diary . . . April 4, 2024

Today was a tricky day. Julio was building and stacking markers during the lesson. It made me so frustrated. I was like, "I'm volunteering to help you all do well. I want you to do well. It is not the time to be playing with markers! Put those markers down." And of course, Julio put them down for 2 minutes, only to pick them back up again and resume playing with them, swinging them around like a baseball bat. I was so angry with him and I was on Zoom. Nothing I could really do. I said, "Mr. Tim, you are there. Handle that!" To which he said, "Julio, stop playing with the markers." Afterwards, I kept Julio and tried to talk with him, but he wouldn't engage, wouldn't even look at the camera.

I was so mad. And then I wasn't. I stepped out of myself and into the situation from a different perspective. Mr. Tim (the paraprofessional) said Julio always gets in trouble. As I talked through the situation with Christine (a trusted friend), I was able to take a different perspective and remember that this wasn't about me. This was about Julio. Julio as a kid who needs help to grow up, act right and possibly even learn enough ratios to pass the test. This isn't about me getting angry. I was centering myself, lost in my feelings at the moment. I know to breathe and listen with my heart so I can hear what kids are saying. That evening, through good conversation with a trusted friend I was able to.

Julio is a typical middle schooler. Wait. I must do a full stop there. What does "typical" mean? Christine asks. What do I mean by that? What is it a code for? How does it further hide Julio? Because this is about seeing Julio, not hiding him under tired euphemisms and old code words that don't help us to reach or teach him. Christine asks me, "When I say 'typical,' am I then lumping/dumping Julio into a box that he may or may not belong in? What do I know about Julio? What do his teachers know about him? How do we reach him if we don't know him? Who can reach him? And how has he come to be defined as 'the proverbial troublemaker'?" How did I, a generally culturally responsible teacher in training for 37 years no less, fall into the trap of just getting mad and wanting to kick him out of intervention? Just like that. Thankfully, at least I also learned how to be a reflective teacher too.

Julio doesn't like math, and he doesn't even try much anymore. I am doing a Zoom intervention. It is a small group. But I must STRETCH my own pedagogy to dig deeper to help Julio. I don't get to kick him out of class. I get to show up and teach him. He deserves that. It is part of the oath I take as a public school teacher. I teach everyone that shows up, no matter what. I have to find the tools to reach Julio. I don't get to kick him out of the intervention session by telling myself and others that it is best because we only have a bit of time and he is wasting my time, others' time, and his time. And I want to teach students who want to learn. WHAT? I want to teach students who want to learn? Don't we all? All kids want to learn (deep down; sometimes, it's buried way further down than most people will look).

Postscript:

> MR. L.: Julio isn't coming today. He refuses to come.
> ME: Yes, he has been having some trouble in here.
> MR. L.: Julio has beef with everybody. That boy even got beef with his mom. You know, if you got beef with your mom, you got problems.
> POSTPOSTSCRIPT: Julio refuses to come to intervention.
> POSTPOSTPOSTSCRIPT: (Julio comes the next day)
> ME: Hello. I am glad you all came today.

Julio works somewhat and we move on.

I move on with a different understanding, because it is seared in my mind: "If you got beef with your mom, then you got problems." All I can think about is how I can be part of the solution every time I now think of him. Who am I to him? How will I choose to show up, no matter how he shows up?

Final Postscript:

Julio resumes coming. I change, so he changes.

Last Day of Class:

> ME: Anybody have any final questions?
> JULIO: Can you explain how to do the coordinate grid stuff?
> ME: (I smile deep down inside) I sure can . . .

****

We wrote this book because of experiences with students like Julio and because we have seen high-impact tutoring change lives.

When we provide small-group, individualized, high-quality tutoring, our students succeed. We aren't just reading and writing about it, we are working with people who are doing it. We have even done a few tutoring cycles ourselves. In this book, we explore how schools and districts across the country can implement high-impact tutoring programs, the strategies they use to overcome challenges, and the impact these efforts are having on students, teachers, and communities. As we dive deeper, we'll uncover how high-impact tutoring is not just a stopgap measure but a key component in the future of education.

High-impact tutoring is a game changer. Chapter 1 explores what high-impact tutoring is and is not. It discusses the terminology that has changed over time and explains the different essential components of a successful program. What differentiates high-impact tutoring from traditional tutoring is key components of time, frequency, group size, and more. We discuss the key components and the benefits. We also delve into some of the challenges that programs face and possible approaches to addressing these challenges.

A key element of successful high-impact tutoring programs is the shared leadership that supports the program. Chapter 2 launches the discussion of establishing a high-impact tutoring program and the key role of the team. Central to this work is the program coordinator and a collaborative team of educators and specialists from the school. Grounded in the research of successful high-impact tutoring programs, we offer checklists for the team and the rationale for programmatic decisions.

Chapter 3 explores the role of the tutor. There is a discussion about different types of tutors, tutor qualifications, and tutor training. It discusses issues of safety, communication, and the need for ongoing support. We delve into the importance of tutors understanding the key role of assessment throughout the tutoring cycle.

Chapter 4 explores professional development, an essential component of any successful tutoring program. First, we discuss the need for onboarding, which requires a series of workshops covering different topics, including understanding high-impact tutoring, priority standards, structure of the lesson, planning and reflection, relationships, culturally and linguistically relevant pedagogy, assessment, and study skills. Next, we spotlight some important topics in math and ELA.

Chapter 5 discusses the very important topic of assessment. Ongoing, purposeful assessment is the linchpin of a great high-impact tutoring program. This chapter discusses universal screeners, diagnostic screeners, and ongoing progress monitoring. Then, it takes a deeper look at screeners that are specific to literacy and math.

Too often, lagging skills are a result of instruction that lacks structure and intellectual merit. In order to reduce the number of students who are performing below grade level and, thus, are candidates for tutoring, schools should ensure that the core curriculum program meets the criteria of high-quality instructional materials. Chapter 6 summarizes the literature on this topic and provides an overview to guide schools in assessing their curriculum. Since high-dosage tutoring is best aligned with the core classroom curriculum, a critical look at classroom curriculum is an important step in improving learning outcomes.

High-impact tutoring sessions should be carefully planned and aligned with priority standards. Tutoring sessions should provide students with the instruction they need in order to successfully participate in the classroom curriculum. Chapter 7 on the math session and Chapter 8 on the ELA session suggest structures and routines that will help make planning efficient and instruction effective.

All of the research on effective teaching agrees that trusting and supportive relationships between teachers and students are critical for student academic achievement. As Rita Pierson reminds us, "Young people do not learn from older people they do not like" (2013). Strong relationships between adults and children also lead to improved confidence, self-esteem, and behavior. Chapter 9 unpacks the literature on this important component and provides suggestions for how tutors can build these types of relationships.

An often-overlooked aspect of tutoring support is working with students on study skills. Teaching these skills can have a significant impact on a student's sense of self-efficacy and achievement. Chapter 10 unpacks different aspects of study skills students need for success including executive function skills, text comprehension skills in math and literacy, writing skills, and test-taking skills. Chapter 10 also reminds us of the importance of connecting school and home, that students need to set up study spaces at home, and to include parents in that work.

Chapter 11 picks up the thread of the home–school connection to explore the various collaborative relationships that can be tapped in order to support student learning. In addition to the instructional team at school, families and the students themselves are key players in this work. Various strategies for fostering collaboration and responding to challenges in building those relationships are discussed.

The book ends with an explanation of how high-impact tutoring fits within the framework of multitiered systems of support (MTSS). By itself, high-impact tutoring could be used as a research based, data-driven response-to-intervention program. By incorporating high-impact tutoring within the MTSS framework, schools can provide a stronger learning experience for all students.

CHAPTER 1

The Power of High-Impact Tutoring

In today's world, education is essential and can be transformative. Yet for decades, we have struggled with the fact that some students learn in opportunity-rich spaces and others face a very challenging opportunity gap (Mooney, 2018). COVID-19 only exacerbated the situation, with the richest schools recovering to pre-COVID levels and the economically challenged schools struggling to get all students to learn (Education Recovery Scorecard, 2024). Even in the best of situations, students learn at different paces. Some grasp material immediately, while others need more time and support. Everyone is looking for how to address the situation that we face around the world with unfinished learning (World Bank Group,

2023). High-impact tutoring has emerged as one of the most effective strategies to address the needs of students who need extra help, specifically by accelerating instruction in ways that all students can learn and have access to grade-level content (Nickow et al., 2020).

Defining High-Impact Tutoring

The terms *high-impact tutoring* and *high-dosage tutoring* are often used interchangeably. They both refer to an intensive, frequent, relationship-based program that accelerates learning recovery. The more established term is *high-dosage tutoring*. However, recently, the more common term is *high-impact tutoring*. As tutor.com (2024) explains, "One focuses on the intervention itself, and the other focuses on its outcomes (What's in a name)."

The National Student Support Accelerator notes that high-impact tutoring can significantly impact achievement because it focuses on individual students' needs and works in coordination with their classroom curriculum. They emphasize that it is not about the actual "dosage" but rather about the "impact"; hence the term *high-impact tutoring*.

High-impact tutoring refers to individualized or small-group instruction provided frequently by a consistent tutor. It takes place at least three times a week and, if possible, five times a week. It is based on caring, authentic, meaningful relationships. High-impact tutoring is very different from "typical" tutoring. In typical tutoring, students have different tutors, they have inconsistent meeting times, they are not working on anything in particular but on everything in general or what needs to be done at the time.

Typical tutoring is unstructured and not really built on strong, solid relationships. Much of typical tutoring is remedial. High-impact tutoring is consistent, structured, and deeply correlated with the student's existing priority curriculum. In high-impact tutoring, students are working toward achieving the priority standards at their grade level through an accelerated framework. By acceleration, we mean teaching all students on grade level while reaching back when necessary to scaffold gaps in skills and knowledge that are necessary to do the work.

High-impact tutoring is about reaching and teaching the whole child. It is about kid watching (Owocki & Goodman, 2002) and making sure we are addressing the students as they show up. It is getting to know the kids we tutor. It is inviting them to be the best learners they can be and setting up the environment so that they achieve.

It has high expectations meant not only to address unfinished learning but also to propel students toward academic excellence by providing the emotional, academic, and social support that they need and oftentimes don't know how to ask for. In this context, "high expectations" is used as an actionable verb, not merely a descriptor or edu-speak buzz phrase. High-impact tutoring has proven to spill over into excellence in other courses as well as positively impacting school attendance.

> **What the Experts Say**
>
> "Tutoring—defined here as one-on-one or small-group instructional programming by teachers, paraprofessionals, volunteers, or parents—is one of the most versatile and potentially transformative educational tools in use today" (Nickow et al., 2020).

Why High-Impact Tutoring?

The benefits of tutoring have been recognized for centuries throughout the world. A well-known Western European example is from ancient Greece, where philosophers like Socrates and Plato provided personalized instruction. Today, tutoring is its own industry. Parents who can pay take their children to tutoring centers, where they work in either one-to-one or small-group situations. High-impact tutoring takes this to the next level. High-impact tutoring offers several significant benefits, particularly for students who need additional academic support. By providing frequent, targeted instruction for up to three students at a time, it accelerates learning and helps close achievement gaps.

Key Elements of Effective High-Impact Tutoring

To understand why high-impact tutoring works so well, it's essential to explore its key components:

- **Personalized Learning:** Tutors can tailor their instruction to meet each student's individual needs, allowing for customized support that aligns with the student's pace. While ideally, tutoring is one-to-one, logistically, it can include up to three students. It is recommended that only actual classroom teachers do groups of two or three or a maximum of four students. Most of the research has focused on face-to-face tutoring. However, there is growing evidence that live online tutoring or even a blended model can be effective.

> **What the Experts Say**
>
> Nickow et al. point out that besides "additional instruction time . . . *customization* of learning . . . 'teaching at the right level' . . . [is of] pivotal importance in shaping education outcomes" (Banerjee et al., 2015 cited in Nickow et al., 2020, p. 7).

- **Frequency and Intensity:** High-impact tutoring takes place several times a week, for at least 45 to 60 minutes in most cases. The minimum amount is usually three times, and the maximum is five times. It is suggested that the cycle lasts at least 36 weeks or 50 hours (Robinson et al., 2024). This frequent, intense work with the students helps them to stay engaged and to keep up with the grade-level content they are learning.
- **Learning Integration:** High-impact tutoring is most effective when done during the school day because students are already there. Results show that there is greater attendance and academic achievement when it's done this way (Robinson et al., 2024). Furthermore, the research shows that the curriculum should align with the classroom curriculum and should be centered on the grade-level standards.
- **Immediate Feedback:** High-impact tutoring offers immediate feedback, helping students quickly correct mistakes and strengthen understanding in real time.
- **Boosting Confidence:** The regular attention from a dedicated tutor helps students build confidence in their academic abilities and fosters a positive attitude toward learning.
- **Addressing Unfinished Learning:** Particularly after disruptions like the COVID-19 pandemic, high-impact tutoring

has been shown to help address the unfinished learning that students are experiencing and help all students learn on grade level. High-impact tutoring accelerates the lessons so that students are scaffolded into the grade-level standards.

- **Highly Qualified Tutors:** High-impact tutoring places a great emphasis on the knowledge and pedagogy of the tutor. Tutors can be paraprofessionals, community members, AmeriCorps members, college students, classroom teachers, or third-party vendors. Tutors are given important professional development throughout the process to help them gain the knowledge and skills they need to be effective. Tutors need a deep understanding of the subject matter, and they also need to know how to teach it to the students. Tutors also have to understand how data anchors the process of teaching and learning.
- **Building Strong Relationships:** Consistent tutoring sessions can create strong tutor–student relationships, which enhance motivation and engagement in learning.

These benefits make high-impact tutoring a highly effective intervention for students at various academic levels (see Figure 1.1).

Figure 1.1 Benefits of High-Impact Tutoring

One reason high-impact tutoring is so powerful is that it allows for real-time feedback and immediate clarification of misunderstandings. A student who is struggling with multiplying decimals can ask questions right then and there. They can get the just-in-time scaffolding they need, which might include manipulatives or graphic organizers. They can ask questions and do as many problems as they need until they understand it. If students are having trouble with reading comprehension, they can stop and get the necessary help at the moment. They can learn new vocabulary, talk out their strategy, discuss new ways to think about a text, and try different things out. This immediate, adaptive support helps prevent learning gaps from widening and gives students the opportunity to catch up—and sometimes even move ahead—at their own pace.

A Data-Driven Approach to Learning Recovery

Research shows that "the average effect of tutoring programs on academic achievement is larger than roughly 85% of other educational interventions. This is equivalent to moving a student at the 35th percentile of the achievement distribution to the 50th" (Paper, n.d., Introduction). Researchers have found that high-impact tutoring can have a profound effect on student achievement, with students gaining from **3 to 15 months** of learning (Nickow et al., 2020). A review of almost 200 rigorous studies found that high-impact tutoring is one of the few school-based interventions with demonstrated large positive effects on both math and reading achievement (Robinson et al., 2024).

High-impact tutoring has been found to be **20 times more effective than standard tutoring models** for math. A National Bureau of Economic Research analysis of more than 100 studies determined math tutoring is **more effective for students in second through fifth grade** than it is for younger students (Fryer, 2016). A 2021 study found high school students can learn **2 to 3 times as much math** as their peers from a daily dose of tutoring at school (Guryan et al., 2021).

These gains are made by obsessive attention to the intervention throughout the high-impact tutoring cycle. Tutors are trained to collect, analyze, interpret, and use the data that is collected on a daily basis to move the learning forward. Students are also taught how to reflect, become self-aware as learners, and set goals based on their data. With everyone working together in intensive and frequent ways, student achievement can soar.

Addressing Common Challenges

Although high-impact tutoring has tremendous potential, there are some major challenges. The cost can almost be prohibitive. Schools must be creative in finding ways to fund the program. The logistics of scheduling frequent sessions also present an obstacle to making it happen. Finding highly qualified tutors who will stick with the program and attend professional development sessions can be difficult. Despite these challenges, many schools are finding ways to implement programs through creative planning and resource allocation. To do this well, sometimes, it requires thinking outside the box.

Summary

High-impact tutoring offers the potential to address the unfinished learning that is affecting so many students. It is an evidence-based, student-centered, powerful approach that can help students make tremendous gains in a short time span. This practical approach of providing frequent, relationship-centered, personalized academic tutoring sessions to students who are struggling can literally make the difference for thousands of students in both reading and math. High-impact tutoring implements an accelerated framework so that all students can achieve grade-level standards and reach their full academic potential. It also provides a pathway to boost students' confidence, raise their internal motivation, and get them to believe in themselves and their potential as agents in their own learning.

CHAPTER

2

Getting Started: It's All About the Team

The key to a great high-impact tutoring program is the tutoring team. The team is made up of the coordinator, possibly an assistant coordinator if the program is large enough, and classroom teacher representatives. The tutoring team is responsible for organizing and monitoring the implementation of the program. Members of the tutoring team should be selected carefully, and the committee should not be overwhelmingly large. Research indicates that five to nine people is the optimum size for committees, depending, of course, on the task at hand (Knowledge at Wharton Staff, 2006).

Coordinator

A successful high-impact tutoring program has a dedicated coordinator. The coordinator is responsible for managing and overseeing a tutoring program that provides intensive, frequent, and personalized academic support to students in order to close achievement gaps and accelerate learning. The coordinator oversees all of the hiring, tutor training and monitoring, behavior management, communication between all stakeholders, tutor evaluation, and program design and evaluation. It is vital to have one person spearhead the implementation and the ongoing management of the program to make sure that there is cohesion with the taught curriculum and fidelity to the research that underlies the pedagogical strategies and/or programs being used. Some research suggests that school-based coordinators are more successful in connecting tutors to teachers.

The coordinator needs time to plan, organize, meet with tutors, analyze and interpret data, give feedback, and converse with teachers, tutors, and sometimes parents and students. In order to do this effectively, you must think about how many students and tutors you have and how much tutoring will take place during the week. Ideally, the coordinator should be focused on the program and not have several other responsibilities (Figures 2.1 and 2.2). They should have an assistant if the tutoring program is large. However, the reality is that schools are more likely to be able to have a coordinator who is dedicated to the program but also has some other responsibilities. Possible candidates for this position include interventionists, Title 1 teachers, or instructional coaches. Administrators should participate in the team, but they are unlikely to have the time needed to dedicate to coordinating a strong high-impact tutoring program.

The Tutoring Committee

 What the Experts Say

"Teamwork makes the dream work" (Maxwell, 2002).

- Communicate with the school's administration
    - Meet with the administration to determine how this program will mesh with and support the school's instructional vision. What districtwide initiatives are important to address through this program? Which assessments will you use to select students and monitor progress? What is the timeline for check-ins with the administration?
    - How many staff members are available to support this initiative? What are their specific skill sets? This will help you determine how many students can be served in a cycle and the area of focus.
    - How does this program fit with the school schedule? Is there time built into the school schedule for tutoring? How many days a week? How long is a cycle?
    - Work with administration on ordering materials and resources needed for the tutoring program.
    - With administration, determine who will serve on the tutoring committee.
- Collaborate with the Tutoring Committee
    - Create agendas that acknowledge the perspectives of teachers and needs of students.
    - Schedule and facilitate meetings with the tutors to track program success and identify areas for modification.
- Scheduling and Coordination
    - Develop and manage the schedule for tutoring sessions in consultation with the Tutoring Committee, ensuring it fits within the school day or after-school hours.
    - Coordinate with classroom teachers to integrate tutoring with regular instruction.
    - Coordinate the communication between the classroom teacher and the tutor(s).
    - Act as a liaison between tutors, teachers, students, and parents.
    - Oversee communication with parents.

Figure 2.1 Coordinator Planning Checklist

- Tutor Recruitment and Training
    - Recruit qualified tutors, including teachers, coaches, paraprofessionals, and volunteers.
    - Plan for and coordinate the professional development for the tutors.
    - Provide training to tutors on instructional strategies, data usage, and classroom management to ensure they are effective in their roles.
    - Facilitate monthly meetings for tutors.
- Oversee Curriculum Choices
    - Coordinate the instructional program for tutoring. What resources and approaches will be used?
    - Review lesson plans and program plans with tutors. What additional support do they need?
- Overseeing Assessments
    - Coordinate assessments and scheduling — pre/post, weekly, monthly, overall.
    - Ensure that benchmark monitoring occurs every four to six weeks.
    - Track students' progress (analyze, interpret, discuss next steps) using data and assessments to ensure the tutoring program is effective.
    - Use data to plan for modifications in collaboration with the tutoring committee.
- Monitoring and Evaluation
    - Provide regular feedback to tutors and adjust strategies as needed based on student performance data.
    - Report on the program's impact to stakeholders, including school leaders and parents.
- Logistical and Administrative Tasks
    - Maintain documentation of the time, testing data, and anecdotal information regarding the overall program.
    - Manage the budget and resources for the tutoring program.

Figure 2.1 (Continued)

- Maintain records of student attendance, tutor hours, and program outcomes.
- Handle any logistical issues that arise, such as space allocation for tutoring sessions, busing, early/late drop-off/pickup.

Figure 2.1 (Continued)

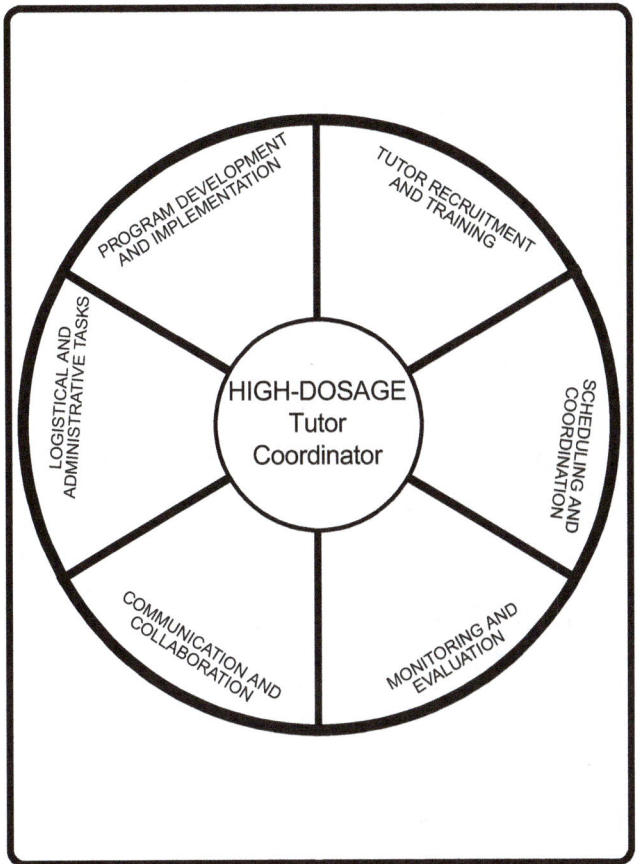

Figure 2.2 High-Dosage Tutor Coordinator

The Tutoring Committee provides an opportunity for valuable teacher expertise and input to be included in the high-impact tutoring plan. The committee helps the coordinator with logistics such as scheduling, data analysis, and selection of students to receive services. The Tutoring Committee should include the program coordinator, coaches, and representatives of classroom/content teachers. The planning process for the high-impact tutoring program is iterative, with one decision impacting others (see Figure 2.3).

> ### 📖 What the Experts Say
>
> A word about looking at last year's data: Remember that every summer, there is a 20% slide in reading and a 27% slide in math, usually larger in math than language arts (Austrew, 2022; Shafer, 2016). It is important to get a fuller picture of where the current student is.

Tutoring Committee Planning Checklist

- Drawing upon the school goals and administration focus, the Tutoring Committee sets criteria for selecting students to participate and creates initial lists of students to invite to the program. When selecting students for participation, these questions may help guide decisions.
    - Who is achieving?
    - Who is struggling? Why?
    - What can be done?
    - Who already gets support?
    - Who does not get support?
    - Who could benefit from more support?
- Designs the structure of the program (when, where services are provided)
- Decides on focus (what types of tutoring will be provided – math and/or literacy – and who is targeted/prioritized for these services
- Determines curriculum and/or programs used
- Paces out progress monitoring
- Reviews assessment data
- Evaluates program with teacher and student input

Figure 2.3 Tutoring Committee Planning Checklist

Setting the Criteria

One of the first tasks of the Tutoring Committee is to set the criteria for participation in the program. The committee should decide this with input from various stakeholders through surveys, interviews, and questions as well as from state testing data and classroom-based formal and informal assessments. All assessment data should be specific to grade-level priority standards and to what extent students have mastered (or not) the priority standards of the prior grade(s) that directly correlate with the current grade-level standards. With a variety of data points, the committee should decide on a focus and on the target population. All students should be given a universal assessment, and then the identified students should be given a diagnostic assessment to get current information to guide the individualized tutoring plan.

Selecting the Students

Once the criteria for invitation are established, the committee has to decide which students should be prioritized for tutoring. Will you target support for students who are significantly below grade level or those who are on the cusp of achieving grade-level standards?

Attendance data is also important to consider in student selection. If there are limited spaces for tutoring, students with consistent attendance are more likely to benefit from the program. Additionally, if the program is offered outside of the school day, some students may not be able to participate given the constraints of their dismissal and after-school plans. The expertise of teachers and tutors and availability of resources may also influence which students are prioritized to participate in high-impact tutoring and the focus for the program.

Another consideration is to think about which students to group together during the tutoring session. Things to consider are the needs of each student and the language of instruction (Robinson et al., 2021). You also have to consider social relationships and behavior. The groups of students need to be socially, emotionally, and academically supportive of each other. You also should avoid having more than one student with behavior struggles in a group.

Communicating With Guardians

Once students are selected, parents/guardians need to be informed that their students are being invited to participate. The invitation should include an explanation of the program and its goals, the opportunities for learning for the student, and an option for adults to accept or decline the offer. Every district and school has a specific procedure for getting parental permission for students to participate in tutorial programs. In Appendix A, we have a sample parent and permission letter.

Designing the Structure

The structure of the program includes the schedule, the number of hours students will receive tutoring, the size of groups, and how students will be assigned to groups. Keep in mind that 50 hours of tutoring over 36 weeks is a threshold of change and that a key element of effective high-impact tutoring is that the students do not miss regular classroom instruction (Robinson et al., 2021). State and federal funds or grants may have specific expectations already established for the structure of the program. These will need to be incorporated into the structure your team designs.

One-week-long "vacation academies" that focus on a single subject have also been shown to be effective. There are usually 10-to-1 student–teacher ratios. The impact obviously is different, but every little bit counts, and doing something like this only adds support to an overall effort. Researchers have found that it is better to have successful teachers do these programs and to pull from a pool of students who need the help but do not have absentee or discipline issues given the time frame (Robinson et al., 2021).

Scheduling

The most effective high-impact tutoring is embedded in schools either during the school day or immediately before or after the school day (National Student Support Accelerator & Blue Engine, n.d.). This is true for a variety of reasons but mainly because the students are already at school, so transportation is not an issue. Transportation becomes an equity question because it is about who can attend and who cannot due to being able to get to and from the school. Programs that are embedded during the day have been found to be the best way, because it is more likely that students will attend. It also doesn't require that students make hard choices about extracurricular activities (clubs, sports, work, and other events). As a second option, right before or after school does make it a bit more convenient for students to attend. Student age and the content focus of tutoring sessions should be considered when scheduling the program (National Student Support Accelerator & Blue Engine, n.d.).

Deciding on the Focus

The committee has to decide on the instructional focus. Will your school focus on math or literacy? If you do both, how will that be programmed? In cycles? By student scores? By teacher skill set? If the team has stronger expertise in supporting math and the resources to structure the program at the ready, it may make sense to focus on math for a cycle while building the pedagogical capacity and resources for a second cycle in literacy (or vice versa).

Deciding on the Curriculum

High-impact tutoring should focus on the priority standards of the current grade. Of course, students will be working on closing fluency gaps along the way as well as on filling background knowledge gaps, but they will do this as they are working on grade-level standards. The curriculum should supplement the core curriculum, not just repeat it or veer far from it. The committee should decide on the resources that will be used and also on how the rollout and training will take place.

A Word About Outsourcing Tutoring Programs

Some schools outsource their tutoring programs (see Figure 2.4). The school may opt to hire an outside tutoring company or use online curriculum programs. If you are outsourcing, you still need a coordinator to oversee what is happening. The coordinator might not spend nearly as many hours doing this, but it is important that the coordinator is engaging in quality control. What is being taught? Who is teaching it? How are they being trained? How is

Pros for outsourcing	Cons of outsourcing
• Programs screen, train, pay, and monitor the tutors • Programs provide a curriculum • Digital systems for tracking the data • Possible flexible times for tutoring	• Cost to doing tutoring online rather than in person • Ideally, someone from the school should be involved in the tutoring • If done through synchronous, remote instruction through a tutoring company that has vetted the tutors, it is highly recommended that someone from the school is there to monitor the quality of instruction and student engagement.

Figure 2.4 Pros and Cons of Outsourcing

student engagement, participation, and progress being monitored and supported? The coordinator should be very engaged with the progress monitoring to make sure that the program is effective.

Summary

Getting started requires coordinating a lot of different moving pieces. High-impact tutoring is worth every moment of effort. It requires time, commitment, energy, and dedication. The coordinator and the Tutoring Committee make critical decisions about the structure and launch the program. The tutors keep it rolling. The students make it happen. Districts should make sure to put a great deal of time and effort into this beginning piece so that the program gets off to a great start and has all the elements of success integrated into its structure.

CHAPTER 3

Tutors

People who work in schools are good at multitasking. We have to be because there are so many jobs that need doing and only a limited pool of staff. Adding a new program to the school day requires flexibility and a commitment to supporting the young people in our charge.

Who Are the Tutors?

Tutors can come from many different places. The research states that ideally, the tutors should be teachers or trained professionals. Using teachers and teacher assistants/paraprofessionals from the school can be very effective (Nickow et al., 2020). Ideally, teachers in your school will provide most of your tutoring. They are trained in pedagogy and are familiar with the curriculum and the students. Research has found that paraprofessionals can be almost 85% as effective as teachers while costing much less (Nickow et al., 2020). It is a natural fit: They already know the school, the culture, the curriculum, and, most importantly, the students. Tutors should be integrated into the school culture. If they are third-party tutors, they should be invited to visit the school to get to know the school culture and to visit the students' classroom if possible (National Student Support Accelerator & Blue Engine, n.d.).

> **What the Experts Say**
>
> "We expect that more highly educated, trained, and experienced tutors will have stronger tutoring skills and will demand higher wage premiums in exchange for the associated impact premium. In other words, interventions employing more highly-qualified tutors will likely be more expensive, but also more effective. We thus expect *tutor type* to moderate the impacts of tutoring interventions" (Nickow et al., 2020, pp. 8–9).

Not all schools are able to staff a high-impact tutoring program in-house. For these schools, there are other options for finding tutors. Some schools form partnerships with outside nonprofit organizations or for-profit tutoring companies. This makes establishing a high-impact tutoring program much easier because the vendor does the staffing, the payroll, the background checks, and the vetting. If the program includes virtual tutoring, you need to consider how students will be monitored and supported. In both outsourced and virtual tutoring, staff from the school will need to monitor student engagement and progress.

Additional tutors can be recruited from parents and family members or community volunteers, also known as nonprofessional tutors. It is possible to pull from the local teacher education college, high school, and community helpers. AmeriCorps, a federal community service project, provides volunteers to work in schools as well. More information on this program can be found here: https://americorps.gov/sites/default/files/document/Leveraging-National-Service-in-Your-Schools.pdf.

While nonprofessional tutors have been found to be half as effective as paraprofessionals (Nickow et al., 2020), they are also free. Since they are not trained pedagogues, they work best in one-to-one settings. One challenge faced by schools drawing upon nonprofessional tutors is that they have attendance problems. By offering a stipend or some form of pay and providing ongoing support, you can increase their consistency and effectiveness.

Especially for nonprofessional and parent volunteers, the provided tutoring curriculum should be highly structured and easy to follow. Lesson structures should be taught (see upcoming chapters), and these tutors should be supervised and given feedback on their work with students.

 What the Experts Say

"A wide variety of tutors (including paraprofessionals, community members, college students, and classroom teachers) can successfully improve student outcomes, as long as they receive training and ongoing support aligned to their incoming capabilities" (Robinson et al., 2024).

Safety

As always, safety is a primary consideration when working with children. The coordinator should make sure that the program is following all of the local, state, and federal laws to protect student safety. All tutors should undergo required background checks and reference checks. All tutors must also understand that student data is kept confidential and that sharing anecdotes about students in the program with others in the community is a violation of a student's right to confidentiality.

Communication

Clear communication between tutors, classroom teachers, and the coordinator is beneficial for the student's progress. This communication must be multidirectional. Tutors need to communicate with the student's teacher(s) to inform them of progress or additional needs being identified. The teachers need to communicate about the classroom curriculum with the tutor to ensure that there is an ongoing link between tutoring and classroom learning. The coordinator needs to be apprised of any challenges and progress that occur. A communication system should be established and should be consistent and planned throughout the tutoring program. This system can be in person or electronic.

Supporting Instruction

The research is very clear that tutors need to be trained and supported throughout the process (see Figure 3.1). The tutoring coordinator should be monitoring what is happening during the sessions as well. Sessions should be observed and tutors given very specific feedback on what they are doing. Many times, tutors are not certified or trained in teaching. They should have professional development sessions at least monthly that discuss not only the curriculum but also pedagogy.

Tutors should be prepared to:

- Attend training sessions — on-site and virtual — to learn about the program, pedagogy, social-emotional learning, and cultural competency
- Review the lesson plan and to follow the instructional plan provided. This can be tricky depending on who the tutors are. If the tutors are teachers, then usually they are in charge of writing and implementing their lesson plans. If the tutors are volunteers or paraprofessionals, they should be provided with a structured program to follow. It is critical to train tutors who are not pedagogues in the program and expectations for tutoring. This is a key difference between typical tutoring and high-impact tutoring.
- Attend monthly tutoring meetings
- Assess and report the progress of the student
- Provide verbal and written feedback on the program and student(s) to the teacher and coordinator
- Get verbal and written feedback from the coordinator

Figure 3.1 Tutors Should Be Prepared

> 📖 **What the Experts Say**
>
> "Volunteer tutoring is not recommended for high-dosage tutoring programs because of the risks of low qualifications and tutor attrition and absences, which would not help accelerate students' learning or support the relational aspect of tutoring" (District of Columbia: Office of the State Superintendent of Education, 2021, p. 9).

Instruction

Effective high-impact tutoring programs balance providing additional targeted instruction in lagging skills and building connections between the classroom and the tutoring session. Tutors should not try to teach everything that is happening in the classroom. Tutors need to be **addressing priority standards** so that students can **work on grade level** in the most needed areas.

One of the main resources for high-impact tutoring programs is the supplemental material that comes with many of the traditional programs. This is an especially good choice if your school is using high-quality instructional materials.

Depending on the structure of your program, your staff may find the lesson plans that come with the curricular program being used are the most effective. Alternatively, a simple lesson plan format that is aligned with the selected goals and curriculum resources can be created.

Take-Home Work

It is highly recommended that students have games and activities that they can take home to work on the different concepts. Games are great because they are easy for parents to commit to doing with their students. They are quick and can provide the needed ongoing practice that students need. The tutor could request that students play the game three times a week with their parents or siblings and keep a log of when they played and three things that they thought about or three problems they landed on and the strategies they used to solve them. The games can be sent home in a personalized baggie, folder, or envelope with a take-home sheet and a form for recording notes and the signature of the parent. Try to make paper manipulatives, games, and resources that students can keep.

Organizing the Tutoring Materials

Part of the success of a tutoring program is the organization of the tutor. The coordinator and committee must make sure that all of these systems are in place for success. There should be a physical and/or digital place where all the materials tutors need for the program are stored. Curriculum resources and lesson plans, general recording forms for tutoring sessions that capture which students participated, the lesson topic, and anecdotal notes, and general supplies such as pencils, scissors, sticky notes, index cards, highlighters, sentence strips, crayons, markers, glue, and folders should all be available to tutors. Tutors who are supporting the development of literacy skills should have access to texts aligned with the lesson plans, phonics manipulatives, flash cards, and teacher resources that support the programs being used. Tutors who are supporting math skills should have access to games, flash cards, manipulatives, and models that support targeted instruction. Some materials will need to be in paper form, while others may be digital.

Tutors can be set up with a basket or bins for their tutoring groups that contain all necessary supplies.

The tutoring box/bag should contain:

1. A folder
2. A notebook
3. The lesson plan or lesson planning book
4. Manipulatives
5. Diagrams and charts
6. A student notebook
7. Pencils, index cards (blank), highlighter, glue stick, scissors
8. Progress-monitoring resources

Goal Setting and Data Keeping

Tutors should have files for each student. They should have a paper and pencil or a digital way to keep track of student data during sessions. After the session is over, this data can be transferred to a digital format so that everyone who needs it can have access to it. Today, with the use of electronic tablets and smart devices, work can be scanned into digital files so that there are digital examples of student work. Part of the tutor training should be teaching how to keep track of their sessions and their data. Progress monitoring is as much a part of tutoring as actually doing lessons.

Using Assessments

High-impact tutoring is dependent upon precise and ongoing assessment. Assessments should let the team know what students know, can do, and understand to monitor progress and plan for next instructional steps. Tutors should know how to assess every day and then use that information as the guide for the next day.

Tutor Feedback

Schools and school districts usually have approved protocols for providing effective feedback to teachers. These protocols typically address the frequency and duration of observations, prescribe evaluation tools that are normed and aligned with the instructional vision of the organization, and suggest formats for providing feedback. Providing similar targeted, impactful feedback on the tutoring program will boost the effectiveness. The chief difference here is that all tutors, not just classroom teachers, should receive regular feedback.

The coordinator needs to monitor the effectiveness of tutors and to provide appropriate actionable feedback to improve student learning. Best practices for feedback rely on descriptive language rather than judgment, celebrate accomplishments and highlight one or two key areas for growth, provide specific strategies to lead to improvement, are given in a timely fashion, and are respectful and safe (Guskey & Link, 2022; Treadway et al., 2021; Finley, n.d.). Feedback should also be based on clearly communicated and shared expectations and is most powerful when linked to student growth.

> **What the Experts Say**
>
> "[T]eachers [and we would argue tutors too] want to know that their leaders, colleagues, coaches, and advisors believe in them, understand their commitment to students, and have confidence in their success" (Guskey and Link, 2022, p. 47).

The most powerful feedback is not only prescriptive (Fink & Markholt, 2011), though that is sometimes necessary for more extreme situations. Instead, when the tutor and the supervisor collaborate on improvement through an approach that uses inquiry into how the vision for the program and student learning can best be achieved, stronger relationships and more sustainable, long-term outcomes can result.

As Connor and Froehle (2022) suggest, approaching observations from a stance of curiosity can help avoid the "fight or flight" response we often have to feedback. Additionally, by posing questions, we are more able to engage in honest conversations and collaborative problem-solving. Through engaging tutors in dialogue, we deepen our collective understanding of the complexities of the classroom context, pedagogies and resources being used for instruction, and the spaces both observer and observed have for learning. "Ultimately, it is the collective wherewithal of teachers to improve their practice on behalf of their students, and teachers, similar to all learners, need to be active agents in their own learning" (Fink & Markholt, 2011, p. 129).

As you prepare your tools for evaluating your high-impact tutoring program, you should think about how you will provide regular and helpful feedback to your staff. Using the National Student Support Accelerator's Design Principles can help you align the feedback with best practices for high-impact tutoring. You can select key elements that are relevant for your context. For each element you choose, generate evidence criteria—what this might look like—with your Tutoring Committee (see Figure 3.2).

Coordinator Planning Checklist

1. Select and assign tutors. When selecting tutors, be aware of the following indicators for a strong tutoring program:

    - Consistent tutors
    - Culturally competent tutors
    - Tutors who can relate to the students
    - Tutors reflect the communities in which the students live (NSSA)
    - Tutors are taught to build effective relationships
    - Skilled at relationship-building and knowledgeable about content
    - Data savvy

Figure 3.2 Coordinator Planning Checklist

> 2. Make sure that tutors have cleared necessary background checks and that they understand that their work with students requires confidentiality. Data is restricted to the teacher and administration. Sharing anecdotes about tutoring with others in the community is a violation of privacy rights.
> 3. Develop and share a policy around communication expectations. How is information shared? With whom? How often? How do tutors reach out for needed support?
> 4. Create a safety protocol for training including emergency readiness drills and specific rules about your school's policies toward having paraprofessionals and non-professional tutors work with students in spaces without teacher supervision.
> 5. Create a framework(s) for a lesson plan that is aligned with the instructional materials being used.
> 6. Prepare resources for tutors to use. These should include classroom supplies as well as curriculum resources.
> 7. Create a protocol for providing feedback. What criteria will you be looking for? How can you include student progress data in that feedback? How often will you provide feedback? What form will this feedback take? In what way can you schedule feedback conversations?

Figure 3.2 (Continued)

Summary

A tutoring program is an extension of your standard instructional model. As with any instruction, support for the teachers is a key driver of success. All tutors, whether they are licensed teachers, paraprofessionals, or other nonprofessional tutors, require a strong curriculum that is aligned with student needs and a high-quality curriculum, thoughtful organization, meaningful professional development, and ongoing, actionable feedback.

CHAPTER 4

Professional Development

One of the biggest lifts is getting the professional development calendar together and making sure that the tutors participate in the trainings. Coordinators should make a checklist of all these things just as a way to keep on track. Some programs require that tutors be able to pass a subject-specific test for the area that they will be tutoring. Other programs simply do an initial round of training, anywhere from two to three days to four weeks, and then ongoing training from there.

Some of this training can be done in a hybrid model, with some being done in person and other parts online. Additionally, tutors can receive professional development through an online course. Ideally, participation can be tracked to be sure tutors are following through on this aspect of the program. Tutors should also take courses in the pedagogy of the topic, understand the standards and data-based decision-making, and take some courses in social-emotional learning and culturally relevant pedagogy.

Ongoing Learning

The most effective high-impact tutoring programs have both pre-program and ongoing professional learning that is job embedded and content focused. Tutors should receive ongoing support in using the curricular materials for the program. This learning should continue to address the research underlying the instruction and understanding and using assessments to plan for more effective instruction.

Invest in Professional Development for Tutors

The school should provide ongoing professional development opportunities for tutors that includes conversations about effective communication, family engagement, cultural competence, understanding family dynamics, and collaborative practices. The school should also set up the templates and protocols for working with families. Tutors should learn how to write goals from an asset-based framework.

Here is an outline of tutor professional development sessions (see Figure 4.1).

Session 1: Understanding High-Impact Tutoring

Session Objectives

1. Understand the difference between high-impact tutoring and traditional tutoring
2. Discuss benefits
3. Get a clear picture of what it is

Session Outline
1. Introduction
2. What Is High-Impact Tutoring?
3. What It Is and What It Is Not
4. Components of High-Impact Tutoring
5. Benefits of High-Impact Tutoring
6. Key Considerations for Implementation (Scheduling, Curriculum)
7. Models of High-Impact Tutoring
8. Q&A
9. Closure and Reflection

Session 2: Priority Standards and Understandings

Session Objectives

1. Understand the Concept of Priority Standards

Figure 4.1 Tutor Professional Development Sessions

2. Identify Priority Standards for Targeted Subject by Grade
  3. Discuss Integrating Priority Standards Into HIT

Session Outline
  1. Introduction
  2. What Are Priority Standards
  3. The Importance of Prioritizing Standards
  4. Identifying Priority Standards
  5. Integrating Priority Standards Into Instruction
  6. Monitoring and Reflecting on Implementation
  7. Question and Answer
  8. Closure and Reflection

Session 3: Structure of a Lesson

Session Objectives

  1. Understand the Structure of the Lesson
  2. Discuss Goals and Success Criteria
  3. Explore Components for Each Part of the Lesson

Session Outline
  1. Introduction
  2. Overview of a Lesson Structure
  3. Breaking Down the Lesson Components
  4. Importance of Closure and Reflection
  5. Integrating Assessment Throughout the Lesson
  6. Practical Application: Planning a Lesson
  7. Question and Answer
  8. Closure and Reflection

Session 4: Planning & Recordkeeping

Session Objectives

  1. Understand the Importance of Planning
  2. Discuss Recordkeeping
  3. Explore Asset-Based Differentiation

Session Outline
  1. Introduction
  2. Importance of the Planning Cycle
  3. Essentials of Recordkeeping
  4. Integrating Planning and Recordkeeping Into Every Session
  5. Planning for Asset-Based Differentiation
  6. Question and Answer
  7. Closure and Reflection

Session 5: Relationship Building

Session Objectives

  1. Understand the Importance of Relationship Building
  2. Discuss Key Components of Strong Tutor–Student Relationships
  3. Discuss Building Relationships With the Family

Figure 4.1 (Continued)

Session Outline
1. Introduction
2. The Importance of Relationship Building
3. Key Components of Strong Relationships
4. Building Relationships With Students
5. Building Relationships With Families and the Community
6. Overcoming Challenges in Relationship Building
7. Question and Answer
8. Closure and Reflection

Session 6: Culturally and Linguistically Responsive Sustaining Education

Session Objectives

1. Understand the Principles and Goals of CLRSE
2. Explore Strategies for Creating Inclusive, Affirming, and Sustaining Educational Spaces
3. Develop Actionable Plans to Integrate CLRSE Into HIT

Session Outline

1. Introduction
2. Understanding CLRSE
3. Practical Strategies for HIT & CLRSE
4. Questions and Answers
5. Closure and Reflection

Session 7: Assessment

Session Objectives

1. Explore the Role of Assessment in Driving Equitable and Meaningful Student Outcomes
2. Understand Different Types of Assessments and Their Purposes
3. Learn to Assess Students With the Assessment Protocols We Are Using in ELA and Math
4. Develop Skills to Use Assessments That Promote Student Learning and Growth

Session Outline

1. Introduction (Why We Do It)
2. Types of Assessments
   - Universal Assessment
   - Diagnostics
   - Ongoing Progress Monitoring
3. Training in the Assessment Systems Being Used
4. Using Assessment Data Effectively
   - Analysis & Interpretation
   - Feedback
   - Using It to Plan Next Moves
4. Question and Answer
5. Closure and Reflection

Session 8: Study Skills

Session Objectives

1. Understand the Importance of Study Skills
2. Discuss Different Types of Study Skills to Use in HIT
3. Plan for Goal Setting and Productive Feedback

Figure 4.1 (Continued)

Session Outline
1. Introduction
2. Understanding Study Skills (Key Components)
3. Time Management
4. Note-Taking Techniques
5. Active Reading and Memory Techniques
6. Test Preparation and Stress Management
7. Test Savviness
8. Goal Setting and Personal Plan
9. Question and Answer
10. Closure and Reflection

Sessions 9 and on
Follow domain-specific professional development for math and literacy.

Figure 4.1 (Continued)

Math Professional Development: Spotlight on Priority Standards

It is very important that tutors are trained in the program that is being used and that this program aligns with the classroom work. Math is very sequential, so tutors need to understand the foundational knowledge and skills that are required that students learn by grade. Learning trajectories are also important because not only do tutors need to know what the standards are at the different grade levels so that they can accelerate learning, they also need to know what the learning trajectory is so they can scaffold the learning. So, for example, let's consider fluency. In most states, the designated fluencies are:

> K—add and subtract within 5 fluently
> 1st—add and subtract within 10 fluently
> 2nd—add and subtract within 20 and 100
> 3rd—add and subtract within 1,000 fluently and multiply and divide within 100
> 4th—add and subtract within 1 million
> 5th—multiply a 2-digit by a 2-digit number

These are necessary to know, but it is also just as important for the tutor to know the learning trajectory so they know the pathway to the designated goal. Following are examples of fluency trackers that help teachers, students, and parents understand the pathway to the goal (see Figure 4.2). Students can keep track of where they

Figure 4.2 Fluency Trackers

are and where they need to go. This helps students to have agency in their own learning, and it helps parents to know where their children are and are going (see Figure 4.2).

English Language Arts and Literacy

Understanding the foundational skills of literacy acquisition is a critical component of training for the ELA high-impact tutoring program. Foundational skills include word recognition and decoding as well as comprehension skills. Once tutors are trained in these components, they should be trained in the curriculum program being used. Tutors can use their knowledge of how children learn to read so that they can use assessments effectively to plan for instruction that follows the progression of learning to read and write (see Figure 4.3).

Continued Support

The initial training is important. Ongoing training is essential. The school should establish systems to make sure tutors know how to look at the data to plan for instruction. They might do it in small teams with other tutors or with the teacher and director. Tutors need the templates to make sure that all of the necessary components are happening and that there is a record of how it is being done. At different points throughout the high-impact tutoring program, there should be check-ins with the tutoring staff that provide opportunities to build community, ask questions, and share practices and successes.

Possible Sequence for PD on the Science of Reading

How Reading Skills Are Developed

1. Chall's Stages of Reading
2. Scarborough's Reading Rope
3. Why Foundational Literacy
4. What Is
    a. The Alphabetic Principle
    b. Phonological and Phonemic Awareness
    c. Phonics
    d. Fluency
    e. Vocabulary
    f. Comprehension
5. How Do We Teach Foundational Literacy?
6. How Do We Assess Foundational Literacy?
7. Q and A
8. Reflection

Figure 4.3 Possible Reading PD Sequence

> Mississippi Department of Education (2022, p. 24) states that high-quality tutoring programs include these elements:
>
> - One- to two-week part-time training session before service begins
> - Professional development sessions throughout the service period
> - A physical or digital reference that offers tutoring best practices as well as scripted tutoring session protocols, exercises, and tools
> - Role-played "mock tutoring" sessions with live feedback to support tutors
> - Routine observation by administration or partner program staff—with dedicated weekly or biweekly time for feedback

Figure 4.4 Elements of a High-Quality Tutoring Program

Summary

Differentiated, asset-based professional development is a key component of any high-impact tutoring program. Professional development must be ongoing and purposeful. The eight outlined topics are important because they cover all the key components. However, it is always important to consider the learner. All tutors need some of the basic information. Some tutors need more training about specific topics. Tutoring should take place before the program starts and then throughout the program. It is important to offer different options; hybrid programs provide more opportunities to get the training done. It is also important to survey tutors to find out what they want training on. A well-trained tutor is an essential component of a high-impact tutoring program.

CHAPTER 5

Assessing Assets, Needs, and Next Moves

Balanced, Ongoing Assessment

Assessment is critical in high-impact tutoring. A high-impact tutoring program should have the goals and success criteria outlined and aligned with evidence-based assessment tools. The assessment plan should be mapped out ahead of time so that tutors know what to give and when to give it. Tutors should also be trained in how to interpret assessment data and how to use that data to plan for what they need to continue working on and what is next. Part of the assessment plan must also consider the needs of different types of students in taking the assessments.

> 📖 **What the Experts Say**
>
> "Many of the most successful tutoring interventions to date collected ongoing implementation data and used it to continuously improve their programs" (Robinson et al., 2021, p. 6).

Three main categories of assessment that are needed are universal assessments or screeners, diagnostic assessments/screeners, and progress monitoring. Your universal and diagnostic assessment tools will help you identify student needs in your building. This "two-stage" assessment plan will help to identify which students need intervention. The universal screener helps you identify which students are potentially at risk of needing additional support. The diagnostic screener helps to identify "false positives"—those students who did not do well on the first screener but actually have good skills in place—and helps you to identify where the gaps in learning begin (Compton et al., 2010). It is important that the universal and diagnostic screeners used are research-validated tools and are consistently used across the school so that data is accurate, consistent and reliable and can be compared and tracked over time. Valid data tools also help schools make more informed decisions about student learning, curriculum, and programs.

Remember that there are different types of tutoring programs. Some programs tutor all the students in the school. Other programs select a grade level or band. Also, there are programs that select students who are working at a certain percentage or have specific needs. Universal and diagnostic assessments are important tools in making these decisions. As the program is designed, the coordinator can use the following checklist (Figure 5.1) to plan.

Universal Screeners

Universal screeners give a general overview of student achievement across the school. This information provides a snapshot of where all the students in the school are in terms of achievement and who might need more help. Universal screeners are supposed to be quick, to assess specific skill areas, to be norm referenced and evidence based, and to be easy to give and interpret—if you need a manual to interpret it, then it probably isn't a universal assessment.

> **Coordinator Checklist**
> - Create a guiding document that articulates types of assessment, dates for giving assessments, and purpose of assessment. Include all three types of assessment: universal, diagnostic, and progress monitoring. See sample in the appendix.
> - Select or create a spreadsheet or table to help teachers and paras understand the data and to use it to plan for instruction.
> - Plan for PD for tutors on how to give and interpret the assessments.
> - Meet with tutors to review data and check in on how they are able to use the results.

Figure 5.1 Coordinator Checklist

These assessments should be given schoolwide three to four times a year. Oftentimes, schools will use information from the past school year as part of the data. Although this is a data point, we must be very careful because there is a summer slide during which students lose some of what they knew over the summer.

Many commercially available systems are used in schools because they provide consistent data across the cohort and are easy to use. These universal screeners are often computer-based assessment systems that capture and report data or one-on-one interview assessments that require teachers to enter data into a program. These screeners are often given three times a year. The results are tabulated and presented in easy-to-use formats, and because the same test is given three times a year, it can track student learning over time. However, even though many of these assessment systems are labeled as universal screeners, they are not aligned with the research-based definition of what counts as a universal screener. They may be easy to use but do not assess the key skills needed for success and thus don't give helpful information on student achievement prospects (Jenkins et al., 2007; International Dyslexia Association, n.d.; The IRIS Center, 2006).

While most commercially available systems provide little more than a snapshot of how students are performing, this snapshot can provide you with a starting place for determining which students need more focused instruction. Your Tutoring Committee should look at this data to determine which students your cycle of high-impact tutoring will target. These students should then be assessed using a diagnostic screener.

Diagnostic Screeners

After getting a general overview of where students are, it is important to conduct a diagnostic assessment for students who are identified as needing additional instruction. A two-stage assessment system uses universal and then diagnostic screeners. A diagnostic screener will help to identify which skills students have mastered, which they are on the cusp of mastering, and which skills need significant support. This information can then be used to determine how to group students and to plan for where to begin instruction based on student strengths and areas of weakness.

You may find that you need a variety of diagnostic screeners. For example, in literacy, you may need a diagnostic screener to assess foundational phonics and phonemic awareness skills. Some students may have solid foundational skills but struggle to comprehend what they read. These students will need to have a screener that assesses their ability to read fluently and comprehend connected text. In math, you might do a screener on basic fact power and then also multidigit arithmetic. These could be the same screener, with a part a and part b. It is important to find out students' strengths around fact fluency, place value, and problem-solving. In both ELA and math, it is important to screen for the priority standards from the grade before to see how students are coming into the grade.

Progress Monitoring

There should also be regular, formal progress monitoring assessments that give information about whether the intervention is working. This data will be used to track student growth and will be used to decide to either continue with the intervention or change course. It can also be used to celebrate growth and set goals with students.

As you plan your tutoring program, you will need to schedule dates for progress monitoring to be completed. Progress monitoring is all about knowing where the students are in terms of learning the targeted concepts and skills. Progress monitoring shows the academic progress that the student is making because of the intervention. It allows the tutor to look at progress toward the goals. The progress monitoring protocols need to provide valid and reliable data.

Throughout the tutoring session, the tutor should be progress monitoring. Anecdotal data, work samples, and self-assessments capture what is said, done, and experienced. The tutor's plans and observations of student behaviors and skills are important sources of data that document progress.

Everything a student does is information about their learning journey. At the end of each session, students should do some sort of check-in. These check-ins can be very short or sometimes longer. A very short check-in could be a thumbs up or down, a quick emoji check-in, or a verbal go-around. A longer check-in could be an entrance or exit slip. Remember that the tutor should always ask questions that get *all* students to participate. It is important for students to check in about how they are feeling about their process and really get the chance to reflect on that. It is also just as important for students to do some work and then reflect on that work.

The tutor should look at the data and measure it against the expected outcomes. It is very important that everyone knows what the expected outcomes are from the very beginning of the tutoring intervention. It is important that the goals and the success criteria are clearly detailed.

When planning progress monitoring for a high-impact tutoring program, it is important to consider the challenges and barriers that might come up in your specific situation with administration, scoring, and data entry. Here are three things to consider about data collection and entry challenges and strategies:

1. The assessments for the interventions should be mapped out ahead of time (assessments, time frame).
2. Scoring protocols and procedures should be very clear.
3. Data entry should be explained and practiced.

It is important to make sure that the data has been collected as needed, analyzed, and interpreted thoroughly and correctly and that you have accurately captured the data so that you can decide the next steps.

 What the Experts Say

"For formative assessments to result in more student learning, tutors need time and support to review the assessment, as well as knowledge of how to address each student's needs" (Robinson et al., 2021, p. 6).

Digital Progress Monitoring

Many school districts use different digital progress monitoring systems. Some of these are great. In terms of high-impact tutoring, I would recommend that the tutor get very specific with the types of assessments that I have mentioned in the chapter. Because we have the advantage of only looking deeply at a few students, we can take the time to do the trace back through the grades and find out exactly where the issues are. For example, a fifth grader who is struggling with division might not be just struggling with fifth-grade math. If we do an academic trace of the subject, whereby we give a division assessment that has problems from different grade levels, we can then determine where the real issues with division begin. Oftentimes, digital assessments are not going to give you the detail of a trace. This isn't to say that the digital assessments can't be used alongside traces, but I would use the digital assessments as another data point.

Kearns (2016) has written about using data collection and graphing with computer software. The Center on Multi-Tiered System of Supports created a data collection system "designed to help educators collect academic progress monitoring data across multiple measures as a part of the data-based individualization (DBI) process. This tool allows educators to store data for multiple students (across multiple measures), graph student progress, and set individualized goals for a student on specific measures."

 What the Experts Say

Center on Multi-Tiered System of Supports data graphing resource: https://mtss4success.org/resource/student-progress-monitoring-tool-data-collection-and-graphing

Literacy Screeners

Research on how we learn to read shows us that we need to assess a variety of skills when assessing literacy. Age, grade, and knowledge of students informs which assessments will help us understand the learning profile of individuals.

The most foundational assessments look at how children understand how books work, the alphabetic principle, phonemic awareness (the sounds of words and word parts), and phonics (how words are encoded in print).

Concepts About Print

Marie Clay created the Concepts About Print tool to assess how readers are building this knowledge (Clay, 2017). Among other things, this tool assesses if students understand directionality from how to hold a book to identifying a cover, turning pages, and where words are located on a page. It also assesses if students can point to or frame a word, find the first word and the last word on a page, and identify punctuation marks. You can find PDF forms of instructions and data collection for this tool in many places online.

Alphabetic Knowledge

We also need to assess alphabetic knowledge (the names and sounds of letters alone and in combination, the shapes of the letters in different sizes and fonts, and the ability to write letters). Students need to have fluency and automaticity in identifying letter sounds and making letters.

Phonemic Awareness

Phonemic awareness is the ability to hear sounds in words. This is an oral language skill. What sound do words begin with? What are the ending sounds and middle sounds? Can students identify rhymes and syllables? Can they combine individual sounds into a word? For example, the teacher says /c/ /a/ /t/ and the child responds "cat." Can they deconstruct a word into its individual sounds where "dog" becomes /d/ /o/ /g/? Can they break a compound word into its parts? We often ask young learners to do this when we ask them to stretch out the words that they are trying to spell.

Phonics

All of the alphabetic and phonemic awareness skills are precursors to phonics skills. Assessments of phonics ask students to decode written language using what they know about the alphabet and sounds of the spoken language. Phonics assessments help us know if our students have mastered specific phonics rules that govern vowel sounds in words such as the silent E or vowel teams. They also help us know if students understand how to decode multisyllabic words or words with prefixes and suffixes. A common aspect of phonics assessments is the requirement that students read "nonsense words." These one-syllable pseudowords assess if students can apply phonics knowledge to new situations. Often, these one-syllable "words" can be found as syllables within multisyllabic words.

High-Frequency Words

There are about 100 words that make up about 50% of the words used in academic settings. Twenty-five percent of these words are spelled irregularly. Effective and efficient readers can read these high-frequency words with automaticity in context and in isolation and can spell these words in their own writing. Schools should select an agreed upon, up-to-date list of high-frequency words that should be mastered in each grade beginning in kindergarten. Student mastery of these words should be assessed to provide important information on planning for tutoring instruction.

Reading Connected Text

Each of the subskills in literacy are an intrinsic part of the overall ability to read connected text with fluency and comprehension. To make meaning from text, students need to be able to read individual words fluently, use knowledge of syntax and punctuation to chunk words into meaningful phrases, draw upon background knowledge, and monitor how—or if—they are making meaning. There are a number of ways we can assess comprehension including computer-based universal screeners, tests of oral reading fluency that come with reading programs used in schools, and running records using standardized-reading passages. Tests of oral reading fluency (ORF) and running records allow the teacher to identify patterns in the errors students make, listen for prosody or phrasing and intonation, and note rate of reading. Computer-based universal screeners, while providing standardized indicators of skill efficiently, do not provide the same depth of data.

Math Screeners

In math, we still struggle to find really great universal screeners. Many schools will give schoolwide assessments three times a year that assess for everything; therefore, they do not give us the targeted data we need about the priority standards. Given that screeners should be short, they should get right to the point. Optimally, we need to know about student basic fact fluency, work with multi-digit numbers in second grade and beyond, and place value. We also need to know about student problem-solving skills. A good universal math screener should be focused on seven elements of number sense (Faulkner & Cain, 2009).

1. Quantity/Magnitude
2. Numeration
3. Equality
4. Base ten
5. Form a number
6. Proportional reasoning
7. Algebraic and geometric thinking

We need to do diagnostic assessments for subskills for students who don't score well on these tests. In lower grades, a math running record type of assessment or interview such as the Math Running Records (Newton, 2016) or the Early Childhood Assessment in Mathematics (Mosseson-Teig & Cunningham, 2015) would be helpful in understanding student learning gaps.

Quantity/Magnitude

Students are expected to learn the meaning and size of numbers. Quantity is a big idea in number sense. In grades K–2, the focus is on whole numbers. Students start exploring magnitude of number in kindergarten through comparing numbers within 10. A question might be: Which one is larger, 5 or 9? In grades 3 through 5, the students are expected to extend this concept with fractions and, eventually, decimals. A question might be: Which fraction is larger, 2/3 or 3/4?

Numeration

Numeration centers on the idea that we have a system based on 10. In the primary grades, students start working with this ideas. In kindergarten, students look at teen numbers as a 10 and the leftovers. In first grade, they formally start looking at numbers and talking about them in terms like 34 is 3 tens and 4 ones. In the upper elementary grades, they should be able to discuss decimals as wholes and parts. For example, 1.19 is 1 whole, 1 tenth, and 9 hundredths. Ma notes that students should be able to explain regrouping in terms of composing and decomposing numbers (1999).

Equality

Students are expected to understand, model, and discuss equality across the grades. In grades K–2, the focus is on whole numbers. Equality begins to be explored in kindergarten informally because they work on ways to decompose a number. They are working toward understanding that 5 + 5 and 8 + 2 all make 10. This is formalized with an actual standard on equality in first grade, where students have to work with equations such as 9 = 5 + 4 and 4 + 6 = 6 + 4. In the upper elementary grades, students extend their understanding of equality to fractions and decimals. A question in fourth grade might deal with equivalent fractions such as 1/2 = ? In fifth grade, many teachers tend to just say multiply the top and the bottom by the same number instead of explaining that we are going to multiply by 1 so that we keep the value of the number. So we could use 2/2 or 3/3 or other numbers that are equivalent to 1 so that we have a different form of the same value (Faulkner & Cain, 2009).

Base Ten

Students are expected to understand, model, and discuss the base ten system and how we use it in operations across the grades. For example, instead of saying "move the decimal," which is not what we are doing because decimals don't move, have the students explain in place value what they are actually doing. Students should understand what happens when we work with 10. Third graders will say that when multiplying by 10, you just add a zero instead of explaining it using base ten. We have 10 times the amount. Teachers should emphasize base 10 explanations throughout. Otherwise, it just ends up being a procedural step rather than based in the math (Faulkner & Cain, 2009).

Form a Number

Students are expected to understand, model, and discuss the various forms of a number. This work starts in kindergarten when we ask students to find different sets that represent specific symbols. Teachers should do extensive work with different representations of all types of numbers as well as a great deal of work on the number line. This is a very big idea that translates across grade levels. Faulkner and Cain point out that if done well, students begin to ask themselves, "Do I like the form this number is in?" They apply it to regrouping as well as to adding and subtracting fractions (2009).

Proportional Reasoning

When some teachers hear proportional thinking, they automatically think middle school and up. However, proportional thinking starts early. For example, as Making Math Moments (n.d.) points out,

> When students begin approaching problems multiplicatively instead of additively, such as thinking that 10 is two groups of five or five groups of two rather than one more than nine, students are said to be reasoning proportionally. This multiplication thinking allows for students to begin comparing two quantities in relative terms rather than absolute terms.

Illustrative Mathematics (2016) had a great fourth-grade proportional reasoning problem about two snakes. It is about the growth of two snakes. One snake was 6 feet and grew to 8 feet in a year, and the other was 8 and grew to 10. The question is which snake grew more. This is asking students to go beyond the answer that they grew the same amount and to think about the two quantities in relative terms.

Algebraic and Geometric Thinking

It is very important that we develop algebraic thinking from pre-kindergarten up through the grades. The eighth-grade algebra problem isn't an eighth-grade problem, it is a K–seventh-grade problem that manifests itself in the eighth grade. We have to give students plenty of opportunities and experiences to explore algebraic and geometric thinking. Teachers need to really think about the foundation they are laying for algebra with the work on arithmetic. From kindergarten up, we are studying equality. From third grade up, we are studying area models.

Reyes et al. (2010) argue that there are six components of number sense. Many of the components are the same. However, they have a few different ones that are worth thinking about in terms of universal and diagnostic assessments. They add:

1. Understanding the meaning and effect of operations
2. Flexible computing and counting strategies for mental computation, written computation, and calculator use
3. Measurement benchmarks

There should definitely be some arithmetic on both universal and diagnostic assessments, where students are assessed on how well they understand the meaning and effect of different operations as well as their use of strategies.

After assessing this information, we can take a deeper dive. What do we need to know more about given the results of the assessment? Remember, the universal screener gives us a general overview of the students in the school. It highlights who we need to find out more information about. For example, if there is a third grader who misses all the basic facts on the test and has yet to be able to solve the multidigit arithmetic problems, this would be a red flag because coming out of second grade, the priority standards were adding and subtracting within 20 and 100.

Summary

Organized, planful, research-validated assessment systems are essential for effective high-impact tutoring programs. Universal screeners used to regularly monitor student achievement provide a snapshot of the achievement levels of all the students in your school. This data can be used to determine which students need high-impact tutoring. A diagnostic screener must be completed for these students to determine which standards students have mastered and which require more support instruction. These screeners should be used to plan for targeted instruction. Once that instruction begins, regular progress monitoring should be used to celebrate growth and to plan for next instructional steps—whether that is the instruction students receive or the professional support the tutors need.

CHAPTER 6

High-Quality Curriculum

Part of the effective implementation of a high-impact tutoring program includes the use of high-quality instructional materials (HQIM). These are resources that are used to support teachers and students in the program so that everyone is working on grade-level content to develop the skills and knowledge needed to achieve academically and to nurture student engagement and identity as valued members of a learning community.

> 📖 **What the Experts Say**
>
> "When students who started the year behind had greater access to grade-appropriate assignments, they closed the outcomes gap with their peers by more than seven months" (TNTP, 2018).

It is important that there is a clear plan for tutoring that aligns with the school's instructional vision and meets the criteria for effective high-impact tutoring. The goals for the tutoring sessions should be based on student assessment data, target high-priority standards, and be aligned to the classroom experience. This will help ensure that the students are learning grade-appropriate content and that tutors have the resources and lesson plans needed for instructional coherence. Given the time constraints faced by school staff, it is recommended that high-quality instructional materials that are research based and validated are used in the classroom and as the framework for tutoring sessions (see Figure 6.1).

High-Quality Instructional Materials in Math

For high-impact tutoring, high-quality instructional materials are rooted in the learning progressions and priority standards. The goal of the tutoring program is to help students achieve grade-level standards by accelerating instruction. In order to accelerate the instruction, tutors need to know how to scaffold up to the grade-level standard so that all students are exposed to and working toward achieving grade-level standards or the designated benchmarks in their individualized education program (IEP).

Evidence Based

The materials must be research based. Tutors cannot and should not be expected to be grabbing random things from random websites and spaces to try and teach concepts. The Tutoring Committee should have all of this worked out, including what will be taught and what should already be planned for based on the student, the data, and the available materials. The point is that there are research-based ideas about how to teach mathematics and that

What Are High-Quality Instructional Materials?

- Evidence based: Framed around the research with evidence of effectiveness
- Aligned to state grade-level standards: Have clear learning outcomes
- Data conscious: A cycle of ongoing assessment of content and language embedded throughout that monitors progress and focuses planning
- Asset based: Start with what students know to decide next goals for the student learning path
- Coherent: Have a sequence of lessons that build on concepts and skills
- Culturally and linguistically affirming: Celebrate and seek to sustain the diversity of lived experiences that students bring with them to school including languages, literacies, customs, and ways of thinking and being in the world
- Intellectual: Content rich and build conceptual and vocabulary knowledge
- Engaging: Contain content that appeals to students' interests
- User friendly: Easy to use and provide implementation supports. They include a full set of teacher and student materials. Teachers receive ongoing professional learning in how and why to use these materials.
- Family connected: A recognition of importance of family participation

Adapted from The Comprehensive Center Network (n.d.) & Hartl & Riley (2021) & Edtrust-West (2023)

Figure 6.1 High-Quality Instructional Materials

they don't necessarily align with what is always being done with students.

For example, many teachers teach rounding through songs and poems. However, we know from the research that rounding should be taught on a number line. Therefore, teachers should be using number lines to teach rounding in their sessions. All of this has to be planned for. The committee has to look up what the lessons are, make notes, supply evidence-based materials, and discuss the teaching plan. We should never assume anything about how anyone is teaching. If we don't ask, then we won't know. Clarity is necessary.

Aligned to Standards

It is really important that the tutoring materials are aligned with the current grade-level standards. Tutors should be teaching from a framework of acceleration, which means that they are focusing on the current grade-level materials. It is important that they also know the learning trajectory of the standards they are working on so that they can connect what is needed from prior grades to "just-in-time scaffold" what might be needed.

How to effectively do this must be addressed in the training so tutors know where to go, what to get, and how to use it when students are struggling with something. For instance, if a fourth grader is struggling with rounding, the tutor needs to know what the third-grade rounding standard was so they can reteach that and connect it with the current standard.

High-quality materials in math would also attend to the 8 Mathematical Practice Standards or the NCTM Math Practices. The materials would incorporate various levels of rigor and require that students reason, think, justify, defend, and explain their thinking. High-quality materials are working toward developing mathematically proficient students who have conceptual understanding, procedural fluency, strategic competence, adaptive reasoning, and a productive disposition (National Research Council, 2001).

Furthermore, throughout the teaching and learning of math, the content and language standards are woven throughout the high-dosage tutoring curriculum so that teachers are always working on language standards.

Data Conscious

High-quality materials are created around the idea that assessment helps us to move forward. Moreover, assessment is rich, deep, and multifaceted. It has to be more than a simple score. We need insight. We need places to stop, think, and consider what is happening. We need student input. We need family input. We need to give feedback that is helpful and feeds forward (Goldsmith, 2003). High-quality materials ask what a student can do and, based on that, what comes next.

Asset Based

The materials should focus on what students know. The assessments should focus on what students can do and then what should be the next steps given those assets. Tutoring is about kid-watching and making sure we see and are tutoring the whole student. Who is this student? What do they know? What is next for them? What is going to help them? What is not helping them to learn? How do they feel about themselves as a learner on this journey? The materials should be checking skill, knowledge, and affect along the way. There should be a path toward a growth mindset woven throughout the materials.

Coherent

In the high-dosage tutoring program, we want to make sure that the tutor understands the sequence of the lessons to build concepts. It is important that tutors are at least familiar with the learning trajectories of the priority standards so they know what the journey is and make big goals into small "chunkable" achievements.

HQIM should make it clear what to prioritize and the pedagogical shifts that are needed to implement the materials. In math, teachers need professional development around the learning progressions of the topics they will be focusing on. The tutors need to know what to look for, how to assess throughout the lesson, and then what to plan next based on the information obtained in the lesson.

For example, the third-grade standard is that students can multiply and divide within 100 fluently. There are steps along this progression—for instance, first learning the foundational facts of 0, 1, 10, 5, and 2. After this set of facts has been learned, students continue working with patterns, such as 2, 4, 8 and then 3, 6, 9 and then 7. Tutors need to know the progression, or they might just teach 0 to 10, with no real reference to the idea of using a pattern strategy to learn the multiplication facts.

Culturally Affirming and Sustaining Pedagogies

In high-dosage tutoring, we want to create and promote mathematical experiences in which students can see and understand math in their everyday life, their community, and the world. We are ever conscious of the cultural and linguistic repertoires our students bring to the learning situation and tap into and use these resources in our teaching and learning. We seek throughout the experience to develop strong, confident, competent, curious mathematicians who believe in their power to learn and do well. We want students to have a sense of belonging.

Throughout the process, we should be consciously checking our own biases and prejudices and making sure they are not seeping into any part of the program. We have to look at the ways we are helping all students, bridging gaps, constructing bridges, and helping all students to achieve and all families to feel like they can help their students.

Intellectual

Vocabulary is an important part of learning math. The high-impact tutoring program should have ongoing work with students building and maintaining vocabulary throughout the sessions. Students should have to use the vocabulary throughout the lesson. They should be able to explain the words in their own language. They should have a personal glossary and use different graphic organizers to get their thinking down. Using graphic organizers in math can help students to unpack, organize their thoughts, think about what they are doing, and explain what they have done (Zollman, 2009). Tutors should explicitly teach vocabulary within the lesson (Birsh & Carreker, 2018).

> **What the Experts Say**
>
> "Mathematical reading is dense, and without understanding of specific vocabulary, many students struggle to understand concepts. Because of the high incidence of unfamiliar vocabulary in mathematics, teaching unknown words becomes central to mathematical literacy" (Lee, 2007, p. 125).

Students should have to make meaning of the vocabulary in their own words (Beck et al., 2013). Use language frames during the lesson to scaffold students into using the academic vocabulary. A language frame might be: *I rounded ____ to _____ because it is closest to ____ on the number line.* Play vocabulary games like tic-tac-toe, hangman, and word-find-and-define as well as board games. Also be sure to use interactive booklets that reinforce the vocabulary.

Engaging

High-quality material is standards based, engaging, and rigorous. Papert (n.d.) discusses the idea of "hard fun." Students want to be engaged in rigorous activity that pushes them to learn something new. When given a choice, students often pick the "tricky one." We have got to get students to think. We can't just spoon-feed them with easy, mundane things in math class. For instance, instead of asking students "What is 20/5?" I'll ask them to give me a division story where the answer is "4." It opens up creativity, allows them to stretch, and at the same time, it is "low-floor-high-ceiling." Everybody can find their way into the problem in some kind of way. High-dosage tutoring has to open doors so that all students can enter into the problems and make sense of them.

User Friendly

High-quality materials are user friendly because they have to be learned quickly and effectively. The instructions have to be simple. The implementation must be seamless. The curriculum should include both student and teacher materials. The components we're using should be easy to understand and easy to use. Data should be easy to collect and easy to interpret so it's easy to decide what the next steps are going to be. We should be able to explain and use the program within a few training sessions.

Family Connected

Families need to be integrated into the process of learning. High-quality materials should have a parent integration component that values and uplifts the voices of parents. Research shows that parents will help their students if they know how to help them. Schools should have family math events that incorporate families in meaningful ways so that their students can be successful. These might include a day every month on which parents can drop by the tutoring session. Schools should also have homework help for parents and guides and videos of the math that students are learning so that they can help their students be successful.

High-Quality Instructional Materials in Literacy

Evidence Based

While the human brain comes wired for language, learning to read and write requires significant instruction. Very few children learn to read and write efficiently and effectively on their own. Cognitive psychologists have learned that specific parts of the brain must learn to work together for human beings to acquire literacy. (see, for example, Dehaene, 2010; Janetos, 2024; Scarborough, 2001; Wolf, 2008).

The foundations of literacy learning occur in the home, where infants engage in social language and vocabulary building with families. Children engage in fantasy play, narrating stories ("Pretend I'm the sister and you are the kitty . . ."), recounting events that have happened, and building knowledge of the world around them. Many children also learn storybook structures and knowledge of books by being read to at home. As children enter school settings, they begin to acquire more formal literacy practices and skills as they learn the alphabet and its sounds, learn phonics, and begin to read (Chall, 1983). Throughout this process of learning to read, children are also reading to learn as they build content and vocabulary knowledge and increasingly sophisticated thinking skills.

Hollis Scarborough (2001) created the metaphor of a "reading rope" to further explore and explain how we acquire literacy (see Figure 6.2). She separated foundational literacy skills into two "ropes."

The lower strand focuses on skills needed for word recognition:

- Phonological awareness is the ability to discern sounds in words, syllables, rhymes, etc.
- Decoding includes the knowledge of the alphabetic principle and the relationship between sounds and how they are spelled.
- Sight recognition is the ability to identify immediately familiar and high-frequency words.

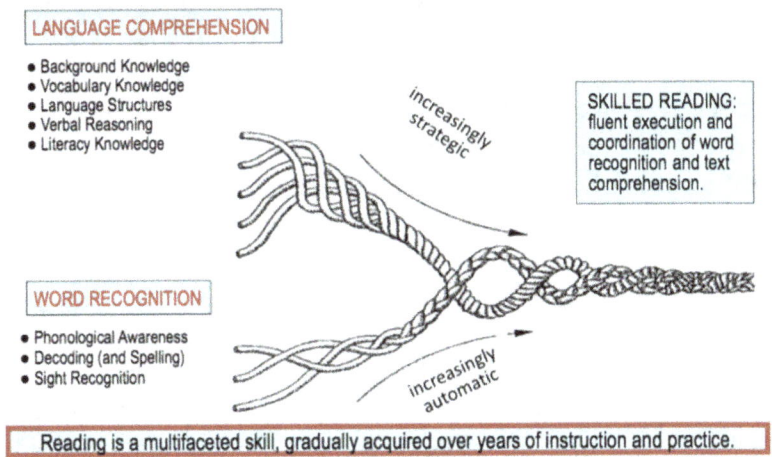

Figure 6.2 Scarborough's Reading Rope

Source: Used with permission of Guilford Publications, from *Handbook of Early Literacy Research*, Volume 1 by Hollis S. Scarborough, 2003; permission conveyed through Copyright Clearance Center, Inc.

The upper strand of the rope focuses on language comprehension. To understand the words on a page or in a text, the reader needs to have:

- Knowledge of the content and vocabulary
- Understanding of the syntax of the language being read
- Verbal reasoning skills
- Literacy knowledge (this includes how books work, genres, text features, author's purpose, and conventions of written language)

As learners become increasingly sophisticated readers, their word-recognition skills become increasingly automatic, and their language comprehension skills become increasingly strategic.

All of this has implications for how we teach reading in the classroom and during tutoring sessions.

Aligned to Standards

Ideally, the curriculum used in the classroom is aligned to grade-level standards, has specific learning targets, and provides students with experiences and tasks that build toward mastery of grade-level standards. The curriculum used in tutoring should mirror what is learned in the classroom, filling gaps in essential skills so that the children can actively and meaningfully participate in the classroom curriculum. In literacy, that means that the curriculum should address foundational word-recognition subskills while also enhancing strategic and deep knowledge of language comprehension.

For most primary-grade students and emergent readers, a program should include explicit lessons in the alphabetic principle, phonemic awareness, and structured coherent phonics. For students who have a solid foundation of word-recognition skills, a program should focus more on fluency, vocabulary, comprehension strategies, and language structures. A key component of vocabulary and language structures should include understanding affixes and how they inform meaning and cognates in English that come from other languages. This could be Greek and Latin roots but also making connections to cognates in Spanish or other home languages spoken by the students.

Data Conscious

The tutoring curriculum should be based on diagnostic assessments that determine student skills in foundational skills such as phonemic awareness, phonics, and sight word recognition and in their language and literacy comprehension skills. If students have gaps in these areas, part of each tutoring session should address these skills. Assessment of comprehension skills and strategies is also critical and should be used to guide planning for teaching vocabulary, language structures, and comprehension of both fiction and informational texts. Because diagnostic assessments will indicate a breakdown point in mastery of skills, students may not start at "lesson 1." Instead, they will start at the point of breakdown. At that point, all lessons should be followed sequentially. It is better to be taught a skill twice than to not learn the skill at all.

Regular progress monitoring should also be a part of the curriculum selected. Throughout the sessions, tutors must use formative assessments and data to personalize tutoring sessions. Tutors regularly assess student progress through short assessments, which allows them to celebrate learning with students and to identify areas in which students need additional support.

Asset Based

Often, when we collect data on student learning, our analysis focuses on their learning gaps. It is equally important to focus on the knowledge and curiosity that students bring to our classrooms. As we build relationships with students, we learn about their hobbies and interests. We can add to our understanding of their intellect and humanity as we observe them engaging with materials and classmates. What do they like to do? What linguistic gifts do they use to express themselves? What questions do they ask? Sometimes, answers to these questions provide insights into skills that did not show up on traditional school assessments. They can also help us to plan for lessons that build on student strengths.

Coherent

By adopting a tutoring curriculum that meets the criteria of high-quality instructional materials, the school can be confident that the instruction occurring through tutoring is taught in a logical sequence that is based on research and aligned to standards.

Culturally Affirming and Sustaining

Culturally responsive practices support academic success while affirming students' cultural identities. When applied in tutoring, they can enhance engagement, relevance, and efficacy, especially for students from diverse backgrounds who may be facing academic challenges. Tutors need to establish strong, trusting relationships with their students. Incorporating culturally affirming practices emphasizes knowing and valuing students' cultural backgrounds, which helps build deeper, more personal connections. Tutors who demonstrate respect for students' cultural identities create a more supportive and affirming learning environment. In literacy instruction, this means that diverse texts, literature, themes, and examples that reflect student histories, communities, languages, and family values should be incorporated in the lessons. Ideally, culturally responsive texts are included in the program adopted for the tutoring curriculum. If not, diverse texts can be added as read-alouds or text extensions that build student knowledge of the world, nurture their identities as individuals and intellectuals, provide opportunities to build critical thinking skills, and integrate a sense of joy and curiosity into the lessons (see Figure 6.3).

Intellectual

In *Cultivating Genius*, Gholdy Muhammad (2020) challenges us to critically think about how we assess and teach intellect in our schools. Rather than limiting intellect to what is measured on IQ tests or the skills students are able to do, she asks us to think about how we can help develop students' intellectualism such that they can build conceptual knowledge, express their ideas, engage in debate, set goals, critically think about what they are learning, and "work through justice-centered solutions" (Muhammad, 2020). Culturally affirming and sustaining education is closely

---

The Five Pursuits

In her model of the Five Pursuits, Dr. Gholdy Muhammad emphasizes that a curriculum should not only build skills needed for success, it should also cultivate student identity, intellectualism, criticality, and joy. Dr. Muhammad asks us to think about these questions as we plan curriculum and lessons:

Identity: How will my instruction help students learn something about themselves and/or about others?

Skills: How will my instruction build students' skills for the content area?

Intellect: How will my instruction build students' knowledge and mental powers?

Criticality: How will my instruction engage students' thinking about power and equity and the disruption of oppression?

Joy: How will my instruction help students to "uplift beauty, aesthetics, truth, ease, wonder, wellness, solutions to the problems of the world, and personal fulfillment"?

Muhammad (2020, p. 58) and Muhammad (2023, p. 17)

Figure 6.3 The Five Pursuits

aligned with the goal of intellectualism. When we bring materials and resources into our instruction that enable critical thought and highlight the intellectual contributions of diverse members of society, we can bring intellectualism into our classrooms.

User Friendly

Often, tutoring programs are added on to the educator's already busy schedule. It is essential that the program adopted for tutoring is accessible and comprehensible for tutors and students. It should include placement and progress-monitoring assessments and lesson plans that are succinct and easy to follow.

Part of being user friendly is having a complete set of resources and materials included in a program. In literacy, these resources include multisensory supplies such as flash cards for alphabet sounds and sight words and manipulatives to help children with word building and spelling activities. Programs for emergent readers should include simple "decodable" texts that are limited to spelling patterns and high-frequency words that students have learned. Use of decodable texts reinforces patterns students have learned, provides practice in segmenting and blending these sounds, and builds automaticity in word recognition. For students who have sufficient word-recognition skills, the program should include fiction and informational texts on a gradient that is aligned with the instructional goals of the lessons.

Family Connected

In all curricular areas, it is important to share what children are learning with their grown-ups. High-quality instructional materials should include parent communication resources. These may include letters home explaining the unit of study and copies of texts read to practice reading skills. Picture and chapter books for reading at home should highlight diverse characters and situations and should be available in relevant home languages.

Integrating SEL Into the Curriculum

Social-emotional learning (SEL) is more than a checklist in a high-impact tutoring program. It is a philosophy that is enacted when we use a curriculum that is based on a framework of "equity-focused social-emotional learning" rather than just a skill-based approach. An equity focus "builds on students' existing assets, lifts voices, promotes empowerment, and nurtures a sense of belonging from historically marginalized groups" (Hartl & Riley, 2021, para 6). By valuing the funds of knowledge (Moll et al., 1992), identities, and skills students bring to the classroom, a culturally and linguistically responsive curriculum gives voice to student experience and ideas and nurtures a student's sense of belonging in the learning community.

In addition to learning the self-awareness, self-management, relationship skills, social awareness, and responsible decision-making skills taught in stand-alone SEL programs, integration of SEL into the curriculum fosters student engagement and provides avenues for civic action. We are aiming to create tutoring environments in which students build strong relationships with their tutors and their peers. Relationships, experiences, contexts, and emotions all matter (Darling-Hammond et al., 2020). Tutors know how to "respond to individual variability, address adversity and support resilience" (Darling-Hammond et al., para 2). Throughout the tutoring program, we are interweaving all of the elements of "social-emotional learning, rigorous and engaging content and precise pedagogy" (Hartl & Riley, 2021, para 5).

Summary

A holistic education that integrates strong relationships, social-emotional learning, rigorous and engaging content, and precise pedagogy is most supportive of young people's developing brains. The curriculum is a major part of a high-impact tutoring intervention. The research states that the materials should be high quality, standards based, easy to use, and engaging. Tutors have to know how to use the materials and understand what is being taught. The materials should be based on evidence about good teaching and learning so that the students can build the skills they need for success in school and life and to support their identities as successful and independent learners.

CHAPTER 7

The Math Tutoring Session

A major part of successful high-impact tutoring is the internalization of the goals for the tutor. Tutor clarity is essential. Tutors need to know what the goals are, what the success criteria look like, and how to get students to learn what they need to learn. Lesson planning should be coordinated so that it is consistent across the school and/or district. There should be agreed-upon templates. The content will vary, but the structure and the key components should be consistent.

Students should know what they are going to do that day and what the criteria for success will look like. They might also check in about disposition toward what they will be studying. Often, tutoring sessions should start with an energizer or routine that engages student interest.

Students should be doing math for at least 95% of the time. Hands-on, minds-on math, thinking math. Math in which they talk, discover things, and are awed and wowed by the world we live in. Finally, at the end, there should be a wrap-up in which students talk about what they have done and how they feel they are doing in learning that concept, skill, or idea.

There are some very specific elements of the math tutoring session. Tutors should know what the lesson plans are. They should have helped plan the next moves based on the data. They should be comfortable with the lesson flow. They need to know what the next steps are based on what is happening in the lesson. If the tutors are classroom teachers, then it is more likely that they will know how to do these things. Anybody else needs ongoing monitoring and training. Many teachers need help with specific math learning trajectories (for preK–3, see Clements & Sarama, 2024).

Anatomy of a Lesson

In math intervention, students should always review operations and place value. It is recommended that tutors spend about 5 to 10 minutes on a fluency routine (based on the designated grade-level fluency), whether it is a number talk, picture chat, or fluency energizer or routine. Also, if there is time, it is always good to do a quick place value review such as a number of the day or a number line routine. After the ongoing spaced practice, the actual lesson should begin.

Math tutoring sessions should focus on the priority standards for the grade. These standards are mainly from the strands of operations and algebraic thinking, place value, fractions and decimals. There are also a few priority standards in the measurement standards. It is essential that the tutoring sessions are focusing on these standards. Tutoring sessions cannot waste the time, nor should they spend the time chasing the teacher around the textbook. The goal is to get students proficient in all priority standards for the grade. This means that sometimes, at Tier 1, they are working on geometry. However, in Tier 2 and Tier 3, the tutor is working on the priority standards.

Here is an example of a Decimal Learning Trajectory. If a student was struggling with decimals, the tutor would figure out where they are on the learning trajectory and then go from there depending on the grade (see Figure 7.1).

For example, when tutoring a second grader, the class might be working on measurement. However, the tutor is working on the priority measurement standard, which is adding and subtracting measurement problems on an open number line. Another example: Say a fourth-grade student is working on angles in the core classroom. In the tutoring session, the tutor might be working on adding and subtracting two- and three-digit numbers and relating

Decimal Learning Journey (For Students)

Get ready to become a Decimal Detective! Here's your mission, step by step:

1. **Show fractions with decimals.**
   - "I can write fractions like 3/10 as 0.3."

2. **Explain how fractions with 10 and 100 are the same.**
   - "I know that 3/10 is the same as 30/100, and I can show it."

3. **Add fractions with 10 and 100 in the bottom.**
   - "I can add 3/10 and 40/100 by changing them to have the same bottom number."

4. **Use pictures to show tenths and hundredths.**
   - "I can use base ten blocks or grids to show numbers like 0.6 or 0.25."

5. **Put tenths and hundredths on a number line.**
   - "I can find where 0.3 and 0.75 go on a number line."

6. **Compare tenths and hundredths and later thousandths.**
   - "I can compare with the symbols 0.6 < 0.75"

7. **Put decimals in order.**
   - "I can tell which of these comes first: 0.5, 0.07, 0.009."

8. **Write decimals in different ways.**
   - "I can write 0.42 as a number, in words, and in expanded form."

9. **Round decimals.**
   - "I can round 0.678 to the nearest tenth, hundredth, or thousandth."

10. **Solve real-life problems with decimals.**
    - "I can figure out things like prices or measurements using decimals."

11. **Use models and drawings to show my work.**
    - "I can draw pictures or use place value blocks to show how I solved decimal problems."

12. **Add decimals.**
    - "I can add decimals like 3.45 + 0.67."

Figure 7.1 Decimal Progression

it to finding the missing angle. The focus is the core skill needed to access the grade-level content.

Lessons should have a variety of pedagogical structures, including concrete, pictorial, and abstract approaches. Tutors should know the tools and manipulatives available for the lessons. These scaffolds should be planned into the lesson. Tutors should have had some training on how to use them.

There should also be ways in which students are building language throughout the lessons, for example, with language frames. Language frames are put out on the table to help scaffold the talk. For example, one might say "The factors are . . ." Tutors should present the vocabulary and the sentence frames up front so that students can use them throughout the lesson.

Progress monitoring should be woven throughout the lesson. Tutors need to know how to collect data throughout the lesson. They should understand that data is everything that the student is doing, saying, showing, explaining, feeling, and more. At the end of every lesson, there should be some sort of short student reflection, even if it is only an emoji check-in.

It is important that the tutor is able to set the lesson within the overall trajectory of the topic. Students should be able to know what they are working on, how it fits into the larger scope of what is being learned, and what it looks like when they can actually do it. Motivation comes from a sense of accomplishment. When students can see their ongoing success, the "small wins," they actually are encouraged to keep going. Students need to understand what the success criteria are for what they are learning.

What the Experts Say

"Success criteria allow [students] to see what they will be expected to say and do to demonstrate their learning and, eventually, self-monitor, self-reflect, and self-evaluate their work toward that end. For teachers, success criteria provide details that allow us to monitor our students' progress in their learning journey. We must have multiple checkpoints along the way to ensure that all learners are making progress toward the learning intention" (Almarode et al., 2021, p. 16).

For example, if I am working with a third grader on multiplication facts, I can give them a trajectory and let them know what we are working on based on their data (see Figure 7.2). Maybe they are working on making connections between 2s and 4s. If we spend a few sessions working on this, and then, when we are ready to move on, they color it, we have visual signs of progress. Bagchi points out that "Whether you are swimming in the Olympics or saving for a vacation, being able to see progress toward your goal will help you reach it." The easier a goal is to see, the closer it seems (cited in Virginia Tech, 2011, para 1).

Students should also clearly see and understand not only the learning goal but also the success criteria. The success criteria let them know what it looks like when they have learned the topic

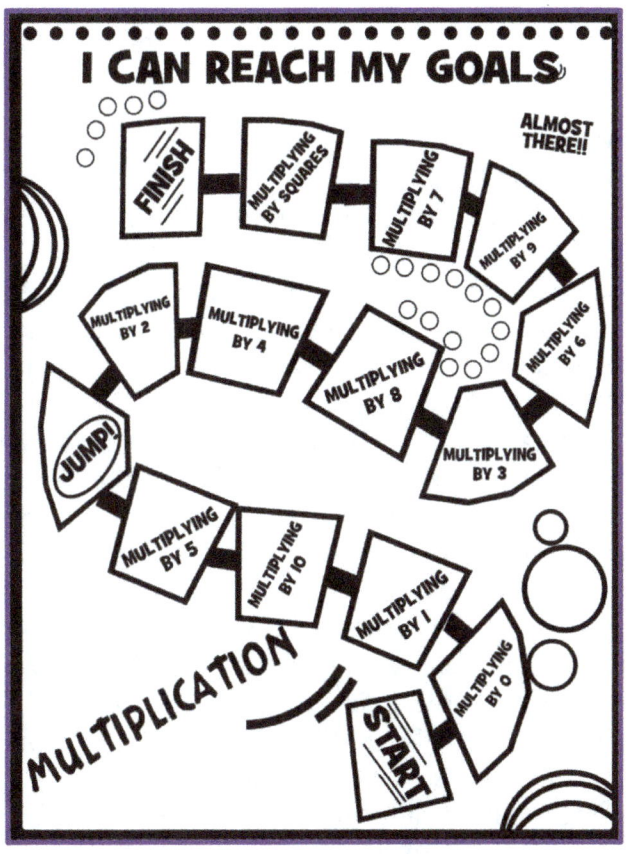

Figure 7.2 Example of Multiplication Trajectory

The Math Tutoring Session | 69

> Week: 4/20/24
>
> Goal: Use pattern to multiply; relate 2s and 4s
>
> Success criteria
>
> I will know that I can multiply with understanding when I can
>
> - Explain my strategy
> - Model the problem
> - Solve a word problem
> - Tell a word problem

Figure 7.3 Example of Success Criteria

(see Figure 7.3). According to Almarode et al. (2021, p. 16), success criteria answer three key questions:

> What am I learning?
> Why am I learning this?
> How will I know that I have learned it?

"Success criteria make the learning target, or 'it,' visible for both teachers and students by describing what learners must know and be able to do that would demonstrate that they have met the learning intentions for the day" (Almarode et al., 2021, p. 16). Hattie (2009, 2018) stated that the potential effect size of success criteria is 0.88, which is well above the average. They further note the vital "relationship between high-impact, high-quality success criteria and meta-cognition, deliberate practice, feedback, and equity" (p. 5).

As part of explicitly teaching study skills and how to practice at home, tutors should give the students something to practice and teach them how to use it. For example, the tutor could give the students these flash cards (see Figure 7.4). The tutor would show the students how to use the flash cards by matching all the parts and thinking about the different representations.

Another example is to give students flash cards with which they are encouraged to think about relationships (see Figure 7.5).

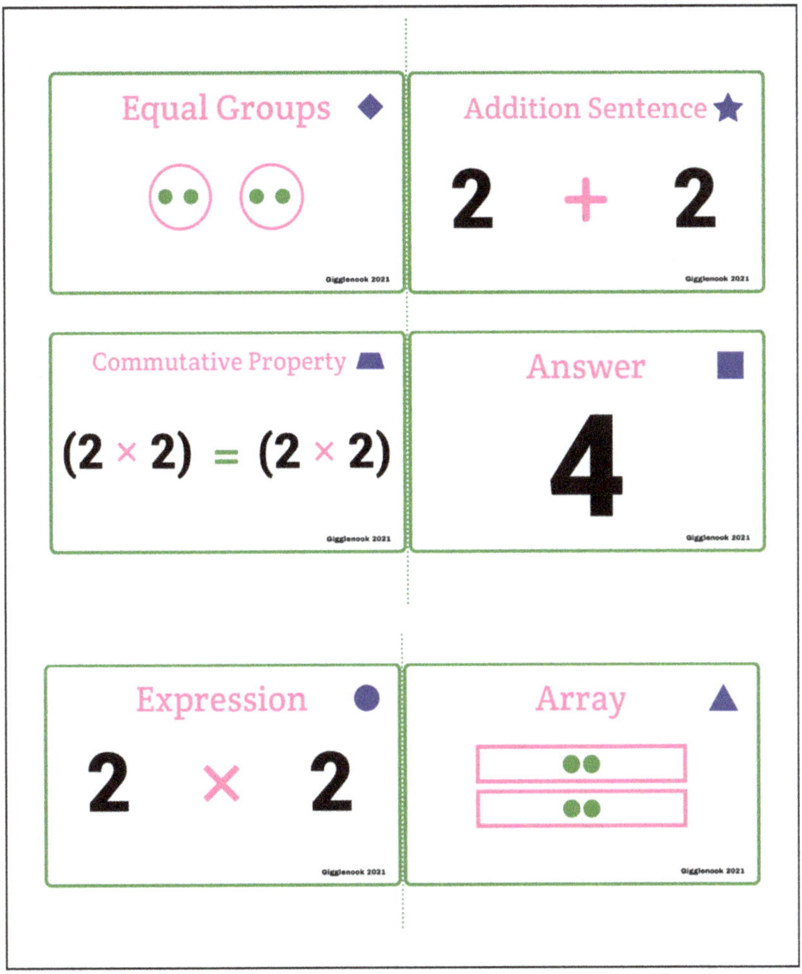

Equal Groups ◆	Addition Sentence ★
◉ ◉	2 + 2

Commutative Property ▲	Answer ■
(2 × 2) = (2 × 2)	4

Expression ●	Array ▲
2 × 2	◉◉ / ◉◉

Figure 7.4 Example of Flash Cards

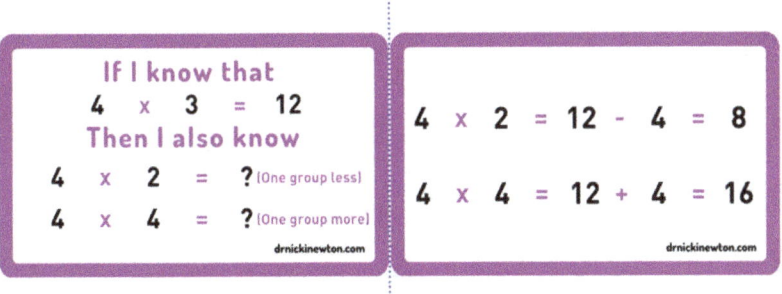

Figure 7.5 Another Example of Flash Cards

The Math Tutoring Session | 71

Summary

The tutoring session is the linchpin of high-impact tutoring. It is where all the planning comes together so the magic can happen. It is essential that the tutoring session is mapped out so that tutors can easily, flexibly implement what is happening. Tutors should have daily session plans. They should also have weekly plans and two-week plans and more. They should also know where they are at least originally aiming to go. That might shift depending on what happens with the students, but they must know where they want to go in order to get there. Everybody involved should know what the goals are and what part of the goals they are working on so that they can monitor how they are progressing toward them.

CHAPTER 8

The ELA Tutoring Session

It is essential that the tutoring session is carefully planned to maximize effectiveness. Tutors should have materials prepared, and lessons should build on each other. As much as possible, the topics learned in tutoring sessions should target lagging skills that are needed for success in the classroom.

Since tutoring sessions are short and time is valuable, tutors should follow the gradual-release-of-responsibility model where the teacher explicitly teaches and models using the targeted skill (this is the "I do" part). The teacher and student then practice the skill together ("we do") before the student practices the skill independently ("you do") (Mosby & Hamilton, 2022). This model has the teacher explicitly explain and then model the instructional goal and then allows the learner to build independence and the ability to transfer learned skills to new contexts. Don't expect this transfer to happen quickly! Literacy is cognitively complex and will require focus, time, and rehearsals to be learned to automaticity.

The Tutoring Session

K–3 and Emergent Readers

Relationship building. As you settle into your tutoring session, you should begin by checking in and connecting with students. The relationship building that happens during this brief exchange is critical to student achievement (see the chapter on relationship building).

Foundational skills. Building the foundational skills of phonemic awareness, the alphabetic principle, and phonics is the crux of the tutoring session for emergent readers. Tutoring sessions should begin with a brief review of skills recently learned or that assessments show need rehearsal. This might be a review of flash cards on sounds of letters, phonics patterns learned, or sight words. Additionally, students should have the opportunity to build phonemic awareness by blending and segmenting sounds. Research in teaching reading to young students highlights this practice as highly effective (Foorman et al., 2016).

Sessions should then continue with instruction of new phonics and word-recognition content. Learning to decode and analyze words through a systematic phonics program has been shown to be highly effective in supporting young readers (Foorman et al., 2016). It is important that students have the opportunity to engage with new learnings through a multisensory approach. They should move from auditory, where students hear and say the sounds, to visual, where they see the sound/word on a card and engage in motor activities like sky writing or writing on paper or whiteboards.

It is important that tutors and students use academic-specific vocabulary in instruction.

Children need to know and be able to use words like "syllable," "strategy," and "digraph" as part of their ability to build on and transfer knowledge of decoding words to new contexts. They also need to understand the structure of narrative and informational texts and to be able to use words and phrases like "character" and "sequence."

Reading connected text. Finally, the What Works Clearinghouse recommends that students practice reading connected text every day (Foorman et al., 2016). High-quality instructional materials should come with decodable readers that are matched to the instructional goal of the lesson. Decodable readers are texts with vocabulary that is limited to the sight words and phonics structures that the students have learned. Part of the reading lesson should include practice reading these texts. Students should read the text independently, with the teacher listening in for application of new and prior skills and fluency. Students may begin reading robotically. The goal, however, is to have them read the text with increasing fluency. If possible, students should take the text they are reading back to class with them so that they can practice reading fluently in class and at home. Research indicates that it takes about four readings of a text to build fluency (Armbruster et al., 2000), so students need to read the text to themselves or to a partner several times. As they build automaticity in calling the words, they can begin to work on phrasing and intonation. If students struggle in this area, the teacher can model what fluent reading sounds like and then have the student try again.

Striving Readers in Grades 3–6

Relationship building. Each tutoring session, regardless of grade level, should begin with you building a positive relationship with the students. You can do this by checking in and connecting with students or playing a quick warm-up game or greeting activity. The relationship building that happens during this brief exchange is critical to student achievement (see the chapter on relationship building).

Foundational skills. Depending on your assessments of student decoding skills, they should receive additional targeted, explicit instruction and practice with sight words and phonics rules. If students do not need additional instruction in basic phonics, they should then have instruction in more advanced word structures. This may include learning about prefixes and suffixes and how they influence word meanings. As an example, many middle-grade students struggle with adding the past-tense marker /ed/ to words.

They may not understand that /ed/ changes a present-tense verb to a past-tense verb or that the /ed/ ending has three sounds: /ed/, /d/, and /t/. Students will also benefit from a study of Greek and Latin roots because it helps to build vocabulary, spelling, and decoding skills, especially as older students frequently encounter complex, multisyllabic words in their reading. Students need to be able to read and spell more complex words. Spelling dictations should be part of the tutoring session. Students should be asked to spell the words alone and in a phrase or short sentence (Vaughn et al., 2022).

Fluency. Reading fluently is not just reading quickly. Reading rate is something we do need to pay attention to, because if students read too slowly, it negatively impacts their comprehension and attention (Shanahan, 2019). If students read too slowly, it indicates that they are struggling with decoding words (support in foundational skills is helpful with this learning gap) and fluency. Reading fluency is reading with realistic intonations and phrasing. When a fluent reader reads aloud, their voice carries the natural rhythms of speech and is able to convey the meaning of the text through phrasing and intonation.

In order to build fluency, students need explicit instruction and modeling in reading by phrases while attending to punctuation. Students can follow along silently while the teacher models fluent reading, or they can quietly read aloud with the teacher. Students should read the same passage several times with an audience (a parent, a tutor, a peer) who provides feedback. Text selection is important for any type of fluency practice. It should be of high interest to the students and have rich, literary vocabulary and structures. Song lyrics, poetry, short stories, excerpts from longer texts, and informational texts are all good sources of reading passages for this instruction (Pinkerton et al., 2017). In order to keep students engaged in the repeated readings of one text, they should be given a clear purpose. These purposes might include finding interesting words, answering questions, reading with fluency, etc. (Vaughn et al., 2022).

Reading Connected Text. The ultimate goal of reading instruction is for students to read a variety of texts with fluency, comprehension, and enjoyment. In order to build this aptitude, students need lots of practice with connected text—texts that are made of multiple sentences, paragraphs, and pages that build ideas around a topic. Students also need explicit instruction in word reading, fluency, comprehension, connecting to prior knowledge, and monitoring comprehension.

> **What the Experts Say**
>
> "Fluent reading involves knowing not only how words work but also how they make us feel. Empathy and perspective taking are part of the complex woof of feelings and thoughts, whose convergence propels greater understanding. . . . Deep reading is always about *connection*: connecting what we know to what we read, what we read to what we feel, what we feel to what we think, and how we think to how we live out our lives in a connected world" (Wolf, 2018, pp. 162–163).

To build comprehension, students need to expand their world and word knowledge (Vaughn et al., 2022) through direct instruction in vocabulary and building new world knowledge through curriculum studies, carefully curated texts and text sets, and connecting to their own prior knowledge.

Students need to learn to respond to questions that have answers in the text, questions that are about the text that may require some inferential thinking, and questions that are beyond the text, requiring readers to synthesize across resources or critically respond to/evaluate a text.

To begin to do this hard work of comprehension, we need to teach students to determine the gist of a passage. As they read, they should stop and jot or stop and talk about the gist of a section. In informational texts, this will be a brief statement of who or what the passage was about and what important information is shared. In narrative and fictional texts, students can learn to summarize the text by using the *Somebody Wanted But So* strategy (Beers & Probst, 2017). This will help them to monitor their comprehension. Can they summarize what just happened? Does their partner agree with them? Can they defend their reasoning? As students engage with texts and each other with the guidance of their tutors and teachers, they will build the ability to comprehend various texts.

Writing in response to reading. Often, state tests are the impetus for teaching students to write in response to reading. But research studies show that writing in response to reading increases comprehension (Graham & Hebert, 2010). Again, specific instruction boosts the impact of this practice. Students can write summaries or take notes on texts. They can also write out personal reflections or analyses of texts. To prepare for this type of practice, students need to learn to spell, they need to learn to construct sentences and paragraphs, and they need to learn how to structure a claim and then provide supporting evidence (Graham & Hebert, 2010; Hochman & Wexler, 2024).

Continued practice. To become better readers and writers, students need to spend time each day reading and writing. They need to have a choice of texts that are high interest and accessible and in which they can see themselves reflected (mirrors) and learn about others (windows.) They should be discussing the texts they read with partners or book clubs. Just as musicians and athletes need targeted, specific instruction and then lots of practice, so do readers.

Summary

The goal of high-impact tutoring is to provide students with the learning support they need to become successful, confident, independent learners. To do this, we need to understand the cognitive processes involved in literacy tasks and then to provide the explicit instruction students need to engage productively with written texts. Students need to have fluent word-recognition and problem-solving skills learned through studies of phonics, to apply the rhythm of language and the rules of punctuation to texts in order to read fluently, and to have a well-stocked toolbox of strategies for comprehending that text—tools such as summarizing, questioning, connecting to personal knowledge, and discussing texts with others. They can draw upon these various elements of the Reading Rope (Scarborough, 2001) when they find themselves struggling to make meaning from text as they monitor their comprehension. If we provide this explicit instruction during the teaching of skills, modeling by the teacher, coaching alongside the learner, and then providing opportunities for frequent independent practice with feedback, we will support our students in becoming increasingly engaged learners.

CHAPTER 9

Relationships and Social-Emotional Support

Why Relationships Matter

Research tells us that when students have positive relationships with their teachers, they are more motivated and engaged. When they don't like their teachers, they refuse to learn from them (Pierson, 2013). Students who have a relationship with their tutors will take risks, ask questions, be honest about their level of understanding, and try harder. Positive teacher–student relationships change student behavior as well as teacher behavior (Li et al., 2022). Positive teacher–student relationships may lead to better teaching (Li et al., 2022). Hattie (2009) tells us that achievement in schools is built upon relationships. The effect size of teacher relationships is 0.72, indicating that positive student relationships are more likely to greatly impact students.

> **What the Experts Say**
>
> *John Hattie's Effect Size Research*
>
> "John Hattie studied thousands of research papers on education to figure out what really helps students learn. He used a measure called *effect size* (specifically, Cohen's *d*), which tells us how much an educational strategy improves learning compared to doing nothing special.
>
> Hattie compared **138 different influences**—like teaching methods, classroom environment, and student habits—and ranked them from most helpful to least helpful (or even harmful). He found that the **average effect size** across all studies was **0.40**, meaning that most educational strategies help a little, but some help much more.
>
> He used **0.40 as a benchmark** (or "hinge point") to decide whether a strategy is really worth focusing on. If something has an effect size **above 0.40**, it's likely making a big difference. If it's **below 0.40**, it might not be as impactful.
>
> In short, Hattie's research helps teachers and schools focus on the strategies that **actually boost learning** the most" Deepseek (2025).

Killian notes that "the quality and nature of the relationships you have with your students has a larger effect on their results than socio-economic status, professional development or Reading Recovery programs. It is not that these things don't matter, but rather that your *relationships with students matter more*" (2021b).

Students need to like, believe in, and trust the people they work with. Many students who are in need of tutoring programs have had a rough relationship with teachers and learning in school. They are often very vulnerable and unsure of the situation. They need positive, affirming, successful tutoring experiences that build both their competence and confidence. The tutor coordinator should be aware of the relationships between the tutors and students. Research has found that "experiencing poor personal tutoring is worse than not having a personal tutor at all" (Yale, 2017, p. 1).

Students have to believe in their teachers. They have to believe that their tutor has knowledge, experience, and goodwill. Maiers

(2021) found that students need to feel that the teacher has genuine care for the student. In her research, these are some of the things she found students want teachers/tutors to do:

1. Smile
2. Pay attention to them
3. Imagine with them
4. Challenge them
5. Ask them about their lives
6. Give them time to think
7. Notice them and acknowledge the things they are doing well
8. Hold them accountable to high expectations
9. Let them ask questions
10. Engage them
11. Trust them

Students are not going to care about the work until they believe the teacher cares about them. Tutors have to know how to navigate the relationship and keep the student motivated throughout the process. A good tutor understands this and knows how to build the relationship over time. Students also have to respect their tutor. Tutors must earn respect by being honest, trustworthy, respectful, consistent, and fair. They have to show that they respect the student and appreciate that they show up and are trying to learn. Killian (2021b) argues that students want their teacher/tutor to be "accepting, warm and nurturing" as well as "aware of and empathetic to" how they are thinking and experiencing life (Element 1).

The tutor–student relationships are pivotal to the tutoring experience and have a significant impact on students' academic and personal development. These relationships have been shown to impact academic achievement, emotional vulnerability, behavior, confidence and self-esteem, engagement and attendance, and overall well-being in school.

Academic Achievement

Positive teacher–student relationships are associated with higher levels of student engagement, motivation, and achievement. Students will participate more not only in the tutoring situation but also in class, complete their work, and push themselves more when they have great relationships with their teachers. When students believe that their teachers like them and believe in them, they will try. They will persevere. They will take risks. They will begin to believe in themselves. Hamre and Pianta (2006) conclude that strong relationships help students to feel safe and secure in school as well as more competent and confident in what they are doing. Students also have better relationships with their peers and have greater success.

 What the Experts Say

"A Review of Educational Research analysis of 46 studies found that strong teacher–student relationships were associated in both the short- and long-term with improvements on practically every measure schools care about: higher student academic engagement, attendance, grades, fewer disruptive behaviors and suspensions, and lower school dropout rates" (Sparks, 2019, para 2).

Several researchers, including Hamre and Pianta, argue that student–teacher relationships must be explicitly planned for in intervention programs. These complex relationships develop over a period of time. Hallinan argues that learning is a cognitive as well as a social-psychological process and that relationships matter (2008). This is why it is important that students have tutors that they connect with.

The student expects honest feedback that is specific and actionable. Rather than just "Great job!" tutors might say something like "Great job! I really like how you modeled your thinking in the problems. Next time, I'd like you to try using the tape diagram." This is an example of specific feedback that celebrates and also gives the student something to work on.

Confidence and Self-Esteem

Research has found that when students feel safe, understood, and valued, they gain confidence and self-esteem, which directly impacts how they act as students. They begin to believe in themselves. They begin to see that it is possible to learn and to make small achievements and get better over time. Students who have confidence in themselves are willing to take academic chances and persevere through the times when they don't initially understand.

A good tutor knows how to navigate the ups and downs of learning something. They know how to encourage and lead students from where they are to where they need to be. They know how to motivate students to try and try and try again. They promote perseverance. Tutors know how to build a student's confidence by scaffolding risk taking, respectfully talking about mistakes as a window into learning, and giving actionable feedback.

A good tutor grows a tutoring relationship with a student. They know how to help students get to high levels of self-efficacy (Bandura, 1977). Self-efficacy has an effect size of 0.92—remember that anything at 0.40 or beyond is a turning point where change is being made (Hattie, 2018). When students believe in themselves and that they have the potential to learn, they do better. For example, "students who believed they would master fractions were more likely to do so, while students who saw themselves as poor readers were less likely to improve their reading" (Killian, 2021a, Strategy 8). Researchers point out that teachers/tutors can help students build self-efficacy by praising them and encouraging them for their strengths and expressing belief in the students' ability to achieve success (Marzano, 2012; National Association of School Psychologists, 2010). Researchers note that for the praise and feedback to be effective, it must be genuine and specific (Dean et al., 2012; Wiggins, 2012). Tutors must help students to set measurable, achievable, standards-based expectations that they gradually work toward, celebrating the "small wins" along the way.

Emotional Support

Tutoring situations have the opportunity to promote *educational resilience* (Downey, 2008). Educational resilience is the ability to overcome obstacles, persevere in achieving goals, and bounce back. Positive encounters between the tutor and tutee foster educational resilience, the idea that students can bounce back from underachievement and dismay.

Student progress is based on strong relationships, trust, motivation, and encouragement. Tutors have to earn the student's trust. They do this by being kind, respectful, and honest. Students need to know that they can be emotionally and academically vulnerable about their learning journey with someone that cares and is not going to make fun of them or think less of them because they don't get the concept the first, second, or sometimes even third time around. Students have to feel that the tutor believes in them and that they can learn. To earn trust, tutors must also do what they say they are going to do and be consistent in their actions.

Tutors who build strong relationships with their students provide essential emotional support. Students who feel emotionally supported can better navigate the challenges of school life and develop resilience. Positive relationships with tutors can motivate students and impact their achievement (Davis, 2001).

Tutors must talk about all the different feelings that come up when learning how to do something. They have to discuss what it feels like to be happy, sad, disappointed, discouraged, encouraged, hopeful, and accomplished. Also, tutors should be honest with students when you are feeling great about how they are working or, on the other hand, frustrated with their behavior or disappointed in their actions. When working in a group of three or four, sometimes, students are off task. The tutor needs to know how to deescalate situations and how to talk to students when they are feeling overwhelmed. Oftentimes, behavior is an indicator that students might be feeling frustrated, overwhelmed, or unsuccessful.

Behavioral Improvements

Research has found that when students have positive relationships with the adults in their lives at school, this spills over into better behavior in the classroom. They tend to try harder. They are more likely to try and follow the rules, show respect to their teacher and classmates, and engage in prosocial behaviors.

Expectancy Beliefs

Students come to tutoring with certain expectancy beliefs—the beliefs in themselves about whether they can or cannot do something (Pintrich & Schunk, 1996). When thinking about tutoring, expectancy beliefs are connected to students' self-concept beliefs—their judgments about their ability to do what they are being tutored on. Student self-concept has a powerful influence on what they believe they can do and how they act. Tutors need to take note of how these expectancy beliefs are shaping effort, motivation, and perseverance. Many times, students who come to tutoring have low expectancy beliefs about their potential to learn something. Oftentimes, they have struggled with the topic for some time, and they believe that they cannot do it. One of the main goals of the tutor is to turn this belief system around.

> **What the Experts Say**
>
> "If I accept you as you are, I will make you worse; however if I treat you as though you are what you are capable of becoming, I help you become that" (Johann Wolfgang von Goethe, 1749–1832).

Goal Setting

Visual goal setting is a game changer. Visual goal setting is mapping out goals visually so that the student and the tutor can see them, discuss them, and monitor progress (see Figure 9.1). Tutors and students must set visual goals and work toward them little by little. Tutors should use the learning trajectories so that students know exactly where they are headed and what the steps to get there look like. Learning trajectories help to lay out step-by-step the developmental process for learning a specific topic. Tutors also have to help students to be self-aware. Tutors have to help students honestly reflect on what they know and what they are still learning.

Motivation to Learn

Brophy (1998) theorizes that the motivation to learn is about being able to find meaning and worthiness in what is being studied. Motivation is a complex idea because students are motivated by a variety of things, and what motivates one student doesn't necessarily motivate another student. In general, students are motivated when they like the people they are learning with, feel like they can learn, feel supported in their learning, and feel like they will be able to use what they are learning. Strong relationships with teachers and tutors can impact students' desire and motivation to learn and achieve. When students like their teachers, they tend to seek their approval by participating and trying to learn. Also, students who are trying to learn something that they are not interested in can be impacted by positive relationships. They can change their attitude about subjects, especially if the work is scaffolded and they

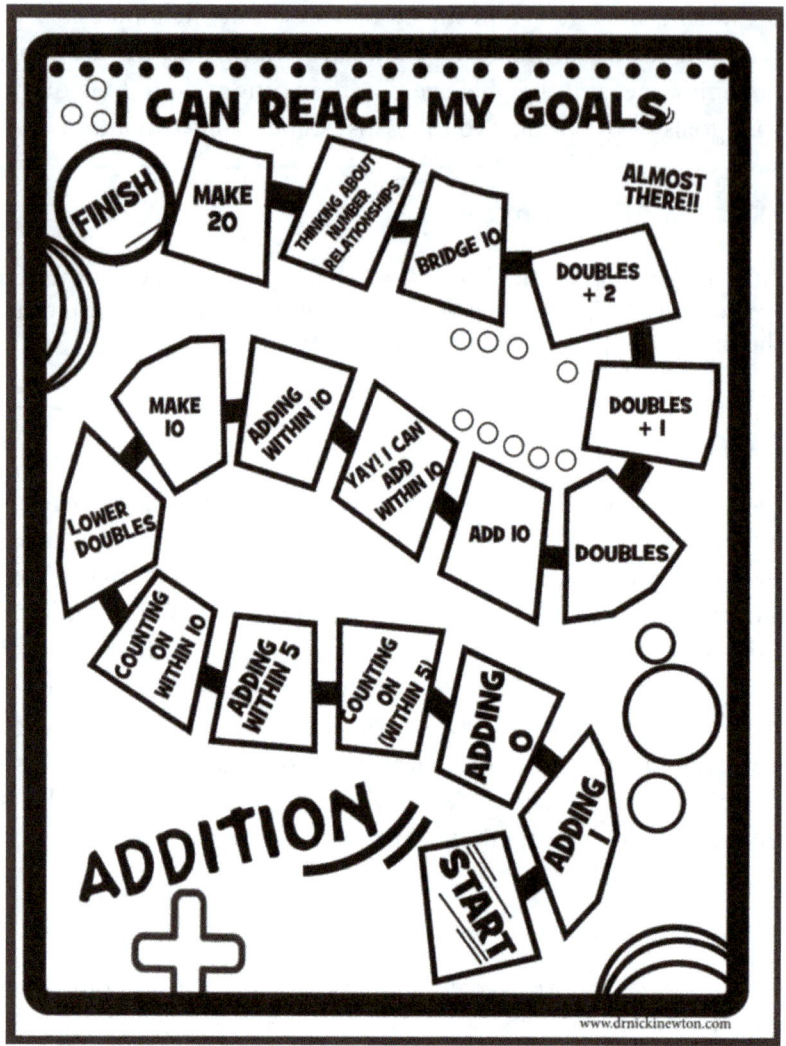

Figure 9.1A Visual Goal Setting in Math

feel like they are making progress. Strong relationships can have a direct influence on the motivation to learn (Brophy, 1998).

Engagement and Attendance

Students who have strong positive relationships with their teachers and tutors are more likely to attend school regularly and be engaged in learning. This is particularly important for students who are struggling in school, have low attendance, and are at risk

Figure 9.1B Visual Goal Setting in ELA

of dropping out. Research notes that we must not only build but also leverage these relationships with students so that they grow across the time spent together (Sparks, 2019). In fact, the existence of a solid relationship can turn tutoring into a transformational experience from a strictly transactional exchange (Thomas, 2020). Immordino-Yang found that it is important to set classroom norms and establish feelings of trust and safety for students but to then use that foundation as a way to promote students' deeper thinking and engagement (cited in Sparks, 2019).

Do Relationship-Building Activities Every Session

Relationships don't just happen. They are planned for. It is important that tutors incorporate relationship-building routines into tutoring sessions. Tutors and students should spend the first few minutes of every session checking in with each other, sharing about their lives and their activities to create a bond (National Student Support Accelerator, 2024). These bonds help to create a safe, caring, inviting space to learn. Talk about outside interests, activities, and things that are coming up in the calendar. They should also play games and do icebreakers to get to know each other better (National Student Support Accelerator). Play fun games like a version of "Would You Rather?" Do emoji check-ins and interesting icebreakers like a whip around the room of "If you were a superhero, who would you be and why?" Tutors should incorporate students' interests and lives into the content in order to connect with students on a more personal level (Hamre & Pianta, 2006).

> **What the Experts Say**
>
> "The magic of tutoring of course seems to be this individualized ability to both diagnose, and hover, in ways that just lead to real progress," noted Emily Freitag (cited in Sawchuck, 2020).

Summary

In summary, nurturing strong, positive teacher–student relationships is fundamental to fostering an effective and supportive educational environment that promotes academic success and personal growth. Tutors and classroom teachers need to have a strong rapport with their students (Frymier & Houser, 2000; Frisby & Martin, 2010). Relationships are built on sensitive, friendly, and honest interactions (Gablinske, 2014). A positive tutoring relationship can impact a student's attendance, achievement, and sense of belongingness in the school. Tutors need to focus on the social-emotional aspect of learning as well as the academic development (Balfanz & Vaughn, 2020). When students feel nurtured, valued, supported, respected, and honored (Piechurska-Kuciel, 2011), they will be more motivated, try harder, and succeed.

CHAPTER 10

Study Skills—"Academic Enablers"

What Are Study Skills?

Study skills are a combination of many different skills that help students with "acquiring, recording, organizing, synthesizing, remembering, and using information" (Hoover & Patton, 1995, para 3). Gettinger and Seibert argue that they can be clustered into four general categories: (1) repetition-based skills, (2) procedural study skills, (3) cognitive-based study skills, and (4) metacognitive skills (Gettinger & Seibert, 2002; Wilmore, 2020). Schools need to take a more active stance on learning and teaching these skills to students to improve academic achievement. Hattie (2009) found that the effect size for study skills is 0.59, which is a substantial effect size, given that the tipping point is 0.40, where we begin to see significant growth.

> **What the Experts Say**
>
> "Study skills are fundamental to academic competence. Effective study skills are associated with positive outcomes across multiple academic content areas and for diverse learners" (Gettinger & Seibert, p. 350).

The Importance of Study Skills in High-Impact Tutoring Programs

Study skills are central to students doing well. The research tells us profoundly that all types of learners that do well have great study skills across subjects (Devine, 1987; Gettinger & Seibert, 2002; Fisher & Frey, 2017). The research has also found that students do not get taught study skills, and so many of them do not know how to study (Nicaise & Gettinger, 1995; Wilmore, 2020). Tutors must incorporate study skills into their work within content-area instruction (Fisher & Frey, 2017).

Several different study skill strategies can be taught. Researchers argue that when students don't have good study habits, they can get very anxious, which can impact their performance on tests (Yusefzadeh et al., 2019). Tutors can do many different things to teach and help students develop study skills. Throughout the sessions students must be actively engaged with the lesson that they are practicing or reviewing. They must learn to pay attention to what they are doing and frequently monitor their learning, what they are understanding, and where they are still confused. They must learn to self-assess and self-evaluate (Entress & Wagner, 2014). Students need to develop "study habits"—skills that will last them a lifetime (Shahidi et al., 2014).

Throughout the tutoring sessions, tutors should be working on building student autonomy so that students are motivated and equipped to learn. One of the big things to consider is the different types of study skills that students need to work on. As tutors are working on these study skills, they must remember to tailor them to the individual learning preferences and needs of their students.

Studying involves a great deal of activity. Students should be talking, working with manipulatives, and explaining what they are doing and learning and writing about the work. Studying should be engaging. Students should be playing and creating games so they can practice and review the content and the skills. Creating games helps tap into different parts of the brain, so students have to challenge themselves to make up a game that makes sense, helps them to practice the content, and then also requires that they come up with the answer key for the game. This type of work helps them to study in a different type of way and requires them to process the information in a different way. Tutors should always be thinking about how to maintain and sustain the students' interest. After practicing and reviewing content and skills, students should be thinking about how they are progressing (Entress & Wagner, 2014).

Teaching study skills to elementary students is essential for their academic success and lifelong learning habits. Many of these study skills directly teach executive functioning skills. Executive function skills are those skills that allow us to plan ahead, problem-solve, maintain focus even when disrupted, self-regulate, and strategize—all essential underlying skills for learning and navigating life. The good news is that these skills can be taught. Here are some evidence-based effective strategies to help elementary and middle school students develop strong executive function and study skills.

Executive Function Skills

 What the Experts Say

"Much like an air traffic control system at an airport helps planes on different runways land and take off safely, executive function skills help our brains prioritize task, filter distractions, and control impulses" (Center on the Developing Child, Harvard University, n.d.).

Organizational Skills

Many students are often very unorganized. Tutors can help them to develop a system for organizing the things that they need to study. This might include labeling and tagging notebooks and note cards in a way that they are easy to find and use. One organization skill is color-coding. Tutors can teach students to use color to emphasize important things and to color-code folders and notebooks.

Time Management

Students need to be taught how to prioritize what they are studying. They need systems for organizing the different activities and topics that they need to work on. They need to create schedules for studying based on when different assignments are due and when quizzes and assessments are to be given. Help students to create a study calendar so they can see what they are doing and set goals to achieve all that they need to do within the given time frame. Time management also helps students to break down their different assignments into manageable parts. It can all be quite overwhelming at the higher grade levels because students have homework for different teachers and topics.

Material Organization

Knowing how to be and stay organized is another part of developing good study habits. Students need systems for organizing study materials, notes, and assignments in folders, binders, or digitally so that they can quickly find and use them. In today's world, it is free and easy to develop online study materials such as flash cards and study notes. It is important to think about who has access to digital materials at home.

Critical Thinking and Problem-Solving Skills

Critical thinking and problem-solving skills are essential in both math and ELA because they help students analyze, evaluate, and apply knowledge effectively. In math, these skills allow students to break down complex problems, identify patterns, and develop logical solutions. In ELA, they enable students to interpret texts, construct well-supported arguments, and engage deeply with literature. Teaching these skills is a crucial part of study skills because they empower students to approach challenges independently and confidently. Integrating these skills into instruction ensures students develop the tools they need to succeed across subjects and beyond the classroom.

Timed Tests

Unfortunately, most state tests are timed, so tutors should practice time management during the tests so that students learn to pace themselves. It is unfair if students only experience a time constraint on the day of the test. They need to learn how to use their time wisely for each section and question. They need to know what to do when they get stuck. Tutors should also talk with students about relaxation techniques such as deep breathing, visualization, and other methods to reduce anxiety during tests.

Metacognitive and Self-Regulation Skills

A really important skill that students need to have is the ability to self-assess. They should be able to reflect on their own learning process and identify where they are doing really well and where they need to improve. Tutors should help students to honestly reflect on their progress and make a plan for next steps. Students need to know how to set goals based on what they need to learn. Tutors can help students to set very specific, achievable goals so they can have "small wins" along the way. Achieving these small wins helps develop students' growth mindset. They see that learning is a journey and that with perseverance, they can achieve it.

 What the Experts Say

"Contrary to the theory that guides some early education programs that focus solely on teaching letters and numbers, explicit efforts to foster executive functioning have positive influences on instilling early literacy and numeracy skills" (Center on the Developing Child, Harvard University, 2014).

Purposeful Spaced Practice Rather Than Mnemonics

Get students to practice and review, because we learn through spaced practice over time. In math, people often teach different mnemonics. Be careful with mnemonics in math, because oftentimes these are tricks that don't actually teach the math. Try to avoid acronyms, rhymes, and word association to remember information or procedures. Students should be given plenty of games that help them to practice and review activities. They should also be given the opportunity to create games to help themselves to practice and review skills.

Comprehension Skills

Effective Note-Taking Skills

Note-taking is another element of developing strong study skills. Research shows that teaching note-taking skills helps students learn to do it well and also impacts reading comprehension (Chang & Ku, 2014). Many teachers do not teach students how to take notes; often, they just expect them to copy them and then study them but never teach how. The tutor can help students to develop good note-taking skills—even if they just do it during tutoring. Students should learn simple methods such as bullet points, diagrams, or mind maps.

There are different approaches to note-taking. One approach is the Cornell Method, with a focus on dividing the paper into sections for notes, vocabulary, and summaries. Another approach is mind mapping, whereby students use different diagrams to visually sort and organize the information. One more way would be to teach students to use a traditional outline method to organize information with main topics and subtopics. There are also many different ways to engage in digital note-taking. If possible and accessible, students can learn to take, organize, and review notes digitally. Tutors should teach students to review their notes regularly to reinforce learning.

Note Cards to Study Vocabulary

It is recommended that students use note cards to write down, highlight, and emphasize important information. Note cards are a great way to study new vocabulary as well as review current words. Students should write the word, add the definition in their own words, draw a picture, and use the word in a sentence and talk about it in real life (Entress & Wagner, 2014; Marzano & Pickering, 2005).

Approaching Word Problems in Math

Solving word problems is a big part of studying math, and it also involves several English language arts skills. Tutors should work on developing approaches to reading, comprehending, planning, solving, and double-checking word problems. While often, students are taught to focus on underlining key words in solving word problems in math, the research shows us that this strategy teaches students to look for the wrong thing and do the wrong operation often (Clements & Bernhard, 2005). Instead, have students read the problem, translate it in their own words, reread it, make a plan, solve one way and check another, and then ask themselves at the very end, "Does this make sense?"

Teach students how to engage in active reading in which they are highlighting, annotating, and summarizing key information in the word problem. This is different from underlining key words. Students should be looking at the action in the problem. Deciding how many steps it will take. Deciding what kind of problem it is. Deciding how they might model it. Deciding how they will double-check the answer. Also, tutors should teach students what to do in word problems when they don't understand all of the vocabulary. As Heidi Hayes Jacobs says, "We are all language teachers" (personal communication, 2005). It is important that tutors are always working on building vocabulary and helping students to reflect on the words they know and the ones they still need to learn.

Reading Informational Texts

Informational texts include textbooks, nonfiction texts, and informational videos and podcasts. Learning to stop and think about texts as one reads helps students to process information more deeply.

SETTING A PURPOSE FOR READING

Before reading an informational text, students can be taught to look at the title and then scan the text for subheadings and illustrations and graphics and read the first and last paragraphs. This practice helps the reader prepare for the information and structure of the text to come. It helps the reader *set a purpose* for reading. "I am going to read this text, and it will help me know about . . ." The reader then should *read*, stop to *rephrase* or jot down notes about what they read, and then *reread* the passage to confirm their understanding. This structure fosters active reading.

ASKING QUESTIONS

Active readers are engaged with the text, frequently asking questions and stopping to answer them as they read. Many students need explicit instruction in doing this. We can teach these skills by modeling our own reading practices by "thinking aloud" while we read. This enables students to "see" the invisible work of reading that happens. Questions such as "What's this part about?" "What I noticed . . ." "What surprised me?" "What challenged my thinking?" (Beers & Probst, 2017, p. 67). As students read, ask them to stop and "Say Something" (Beers, 2003).

TEACHING INFERENCE AND MAKING CONNECTIONS

While reading, the reader stops and summarizes what the text says (It says) and then responds to that bit of information with their own understanding of the topic (I say). The reader can raise the complexity of reading by then adding, "*and so . . .*" which leads to building inferences about the text. This strategy works with texts that come with specific questions, for reading for research, or for reading for curiosity (Beers, 2003).

READING NARRATIVE TEXTS

Struggling readers often expend significant cognitive energy on decoding and reading fluency, leaving little space for attending to what is happening in the story.

RETELLING AND SUMMARIZING

Students need specific instruction in retelling events and thinking about character change. A quick summary strategy for narrative texts is to complete the prompts, "Somebody wanted . . ., But . . ., So . . . ., Then . . ." This strategy can be used to summarize chapters and complete texts that tell a story—fictional or informational. It also sets readers up to begin to understand character development and to track where characters learn and grow across a narrative.

Writing Skills

We write for different purposes. We write to express ourselves, to inform, instruct, or persuade, and we write to learn. Writing to learn is a study skill that can help students make sense of information, to critically analyze, and to build deeper and more meaningful connections to what one is learning. However, because writing is one of the most cognitively complex tasks we engage in, we need to explicitly teach students skills in writing.

Students can use writing as a study skill in many disciplines. Writing tasks in literacy and content areas often ask students to respond to literature and/or informational texts in very specific ways. Students need to learn to respond to the prompt and then provide evidence from the text to support their reasoning. However, writing to learn can be structured to deepen student learning and as a study strategy. Specifically, if students use writing tasks to practice retrieving information and elaborating on ideas by generating examples or answering why or how, there appears to be a positive impact on learning (Wechsler, 2024). We can reduce the cognitive load of writing for elementary students by providing sentence stems and word banks. We can also teach students to create basic outlines and to use graphic organizers to structure their thinking.

Communication and reasoning are two of the process standards in mathematics. Students are often asked to explain their reasoning orally in math class. This oral reasoning and discussion can be the springboard for students to begin to explain their mathematical thinking in writing. Tutors should help students to be able to describe, defend, support, explain, and reason about their thinking. This can happen orally first, and then, with support, students can begin to write out their reasoning. Students need to learn how to organize their thoughts, explain in a logical order what they did, and then be able to defend what they did using "first," "then," and "next" sequencing words, incorporating mathematical vocabulary, and using models to help express their understanding of mathematical concepts. As they finish drafting this work, they should be taught how to edit and proofread what they have written and ask themselves, "Does this make sense?"

Test-Taking Skills

Tutors should teach students how to navigate quizzes and exams. Tutors teach students not only the content but also the architecture of quizzes and exams in general. You need to ask students a variety of questions to get them to think about what they are being asked to do and then discuss the answers so that they understand how to navigate tests. Tests can cause a great deal of anxiety, so we have to give students the tools to take tests confidently (see Figure 10.1).

All of these conversations take place during the tutoring sessions. Students should be confident, competent learners who are comfortable with being tested. They should know the format and the types of questions. Tutors should give practice quizzes and tests throughout the sessions. They should discuss the correct and the incorrect answers. They should have students make their own practice tests as well.

The test challenge	What would children say is their strategy?	What the tutor can say
What should you do when you get stuck on one question?	"I dunno." "Guess."	Try to eliminate the ones that are incorrect. Think about what is left. Pick one. Don't leave anything blank. Give a thinking guess. Don't spend a great deal of time on any one question. Keep moving through the test. If it is a bubble test, lightly circle the question on your test paper and then go back at the end of the test to see if you can answer it. Sometimes, you will be reminded of the answer as you work on other questions.
How do you approach multiple-choice problems?	"I have answered a lot of A's. I think it is time for a B."	Work out the problem on paper. Look for the ones that you know are incorrect. Find the one that you think must be correct.
How do you write extended-response answers?	"I just write a lot. I will get something right."	Turn the question into an answer stem. Literacy: Locate at least one piece of evidence in the text to answer the question. It is better to find two pieces of evidence. Restate your answer in new words as a conclusion. Math: Describe your steps, and try to use at least one math vocabulary word related to the problem.

Figure 10.1 Supporting Strategic Test-Taking

How do you prove what you know when asked?	"I just saw it's right." "I did it in my brain." "I just know it."	In math: You have to talk about what you did. Tell us what you did step by step. Tell us why the answer is correct. Literacy: Look back into the text. Can you find the words from the question in the text? You can quote or restate that information in your answer.
How do you calm your mind before a quiz?	"I get nervous." "My stomach hurts." "My head hurts."	Breathe deeply. Take three deep belly breaths. Positive self-talk. "I can do this." "I studied hard." Visualization. "Imagine yourself knowing the answers and doing really well."
How do you use your time during a test?	"I get scared because it goes fast." "I get tired." "I look at the clock."	You have to pace yourself. Don't spend too much time on any one problem. Skip ones that are taking too long and go back at the end to answer those.

Figure 10.1 (Continued)

Test Savviness

All students deserve to know what they will be tested on so that they can prepare for it. Part of test prep involves knowing the testing vocabulary, infrastructure, how problems are set up, and how answers are expected to be given (one answer, two answers, or even more). Throughout the tutoring sessions, tutors should be showing students problems from the state test so that students learn to navigate the test. It is unfair if the first time a student sees the structure is on the day of the test. This is not to say that tutoring should turn into a "test-prep frenzy." It shouldn't. We do need to make sure that our students are familiar with the structure of the test and strategies for answering different types of questions.

Working With Parents

Parents should know how to help their children work toward their goals at home. This includes helping parents/guardians to think about homework and study habits. Key habits include setting up homework routines so that there is a consistent time and place to do the homework and creating a specific study space that is quiet and study ready. When possible, the school can help parents to know how to use technology, such as educational apps and tools to review skills and study concepts, to support their students' study skills.

Summary

Study skills can be game changers. Although many variables contribute to student achievement, including motivation, interest, prior knowledge, relaxation, teaching, materials, and students' cognitive capabilities, researchers note that a large contributing factor to students' performance is their general study skills and habits (Shahidi et al., 2014). Gettinger and Seibert (2002) note that it is not only the knowledge but also the application of study skills that makes the difference. Since schools have done very little in the way of teaching these skills, academic high-impact tutors should definitely integrate it into their work. As the research notes, there should be an intentional effort to teach study skills in schools (Adams et al., 1982). Students can learn skills that will last them throughout their academic studies.

CHAPTER 11

Fostering Collaborative Connections

Introduction: The Power of a Supportive Network

It is an old but true adage that it takes a village to raise a child. Ensuring student achievement for *all* students relies on a robust network of support involving teachers, tutors, students, families, and support staff. As Maxwell stated at the turn of this century, teamwork is essential (2002). In the tutoring program, we need all of these entities working together. We must build strong working relationships that center the student within the network of support. In designing an effective tutoring program, we have to think about different ways to foster collaboration to strengthen these essential relationships so that we are the most effective that we can be.

A comprehensive network of support that includes all of the players ensures that the students receive consistent, connected guidance, encouragement, and support both inside and outside of the school, positioning the student for the best possibility of success. It pays off to foster strong, collaborative, communicative relationships in which everyone knows the goals and helps in working toward them.

The Role of Teachers, Tutors, Families, and Support Staff

The Teacher

The classroom teacher is the linchpin in the system. The classroom teacher sees the most complete academic picture of the student. The teacher is responsible for the teaching and learning of the priority material. The teacher must work together with the tutor to know how the instruction is being delivered both in class and during the tutoring session so that they both can strategize about the best way for the student to learn. The teacher and the tutor should work together on the priority standards that students need help with as well as an emphasis on achieving grade-level math fluency. The ongoing assessment system needs to be discussed between the teacher and the tutor at least every two to three weeks. This communication can be done face to face, by phone, or by email.

The Tutor

Sometimes, the teacher and the tutor are the same person. Other times, they are not. In many cases, they are not, so it is essential that everyone is in purposeful communication with each other. The tutor is working *only* on priority standards. The tutor might be doing some homework help, possibly, but that is not the purpose of high-impact tutoring. Tutors who are working with students who are struggling with math are trying to catch students up to grade level. The focus is on knowing the priority standards and the standards that lead up to those priority standards as well as focusing on achieving grade-level fluency. The tutor should be working with the student and communicating with the teacher, the parents, and the tutoring coordinator to keep everyone in the loop of what is happening.

Tutors provide personalized instruction and academic support tailored to individual student needs. Their role includes identifying academic strengths and understanding the learning gaps, reinforcing classroom instruction around the priority standards, helping with homework (sometimes, but not primarily), and preparing students for exams. Tutors also encourage, build confidence, and motivate students.

Families

The partnership between tutors and parents is critical in supporting students' academic progress and overall well-being. When tutors and parents work collaboratively, they can provide consistent support, reinforce learning, and address individual student needs effectively. This partnership plays a pivotal role in enhancing student achievement and fostering a supportive learning environment. Families provide emotional, social, and academic support to students.

 What the Experts Say

"Most families want to talk with, monitor, encourage, and guide their children as students, but many say they need more information from the schools about how to help their children at home" (Epstein & Vorhis, 2002, p. 291).

Research shows that when parents are involved, it impacts student achievement (Epstein & Vorhis, 2002). When teachers and tutors specifically tell parents ways to help their children, they will. Researchers found that students improve in both reading and math. They state that in-person meetings, communication between school and home about performance, and sending materials home impact student performance (Henderson & Mapp, 2002; Hoover-Dempsey & Sandler, 1997).

Families want their children to succeed. Sometimes, they just don't know how to effectively support the work. It is important to be very specific. For example, it is one thing to send a letter home telling parents that the class is working on multiplication. This could lead to timed tests, tears, and a great deal of anxiety. It is another thing to send a letter home explaining what fluency means, how children grow in their ability to read different books, and asking parents/guardians to help in very specific ways, such as playing a targeted game of cards working on multiplying by 2 (see Figures 11.1, 11.2, 11.3). Research tells us the power of parental involvement. It can lead to improved academic outcomes, better behavior, and increased motivation. Effectively looping parents into the network in their home languages in meaningful ways that foster involvement can be a game changer.

Dear Families,

We are studying our basic math facts. Research shows that learning math facts includes 3 elements; accuracy, flexibility and efficiency.

Accuracy: We want all of our students to know the correct answer. They learn the facts by practicing them through a variety of activities.

Flexibility: We will be playing several games to build flexibility. We want students to have number sense. We want them to think about and be flexible with numbers. This means that we will work on our facts through strategies rather than rote memorization.

Efficiency: Efficiency means that students can pick quick ways to arrive at the answers based on the numbers that they are using.

* Students will learn the facts as they practice them. With practice over time, they will develop instant recall. Instant recall is a result of meaningful practice over time.*

Your child is working on _____ facts.
In this pack you will find 2 things to practice:
1) Flashcards
2) Board Game

Figure 11.1 Letter to Families

Figure 11.2 Math Game Board

Parents are integral to creating a conducive learning environment at home. Their responsibilities include providing emotional support, establishing routines, monitoring academic progress, and communicating with teachers and tutors. Active parental involvement is linked to higher academic achievement and improved student behavior. When tutors and parents collaborate, students receive consistent messages and support. This alignment helps reinforce learning objectives and ensures that students understand and complete their assignments.

The Student

Students should be directly involved in the communication with their families about how they are doing, what they are doing well, what the next academic goals are, and how they are going to collaboratively work toward them. This approach fosters a sense of ownership and responsibility. Students who feel supported by their tutors, teachers, and families are much more likely to be and stay motivated, engaged, and persistent in pursuit of their academic goals.

Matching Books to Readers

We want students to find joy and fulfillment in reading. To do this, we help them select from a range of genres – realistic fiction, fantasy, science fiction, informational texts, poetry, etc.– and help them build the foundational literacy skills and love of reading and learning.

As children learn to read, they go from reading books with very simple words to long chapter books. At all points in their learning, our young people benefit from being exposed to books that they might not be able to read themselves. Audiobooks and being read to are important tools we can use to help nurture our learners.

Emergent readers are just beginning to understand that words are made of sounds, that letters represent these sounds and combine to create words that have meaning, that each word is defined by space on the page, and that we typically read from left to right and top to bottom in English. Readers at this stage typically use their fingers to point to individual words as they train their eyes to sweep across the page. *Have You Seen My Cat?* by Eric Carle is an example of an emergent book.

Early readers are those who have figured out for the most part how books and words work. They can read high frequency words with increasing ease and use their letter-sound knowledge to figure out new words while reading. Early readers also use knowledge of how words and books work, together with their knowledge of the world, to monitor their comprehension. They read less complex texts fluently and use punctuation to help with phrasing. Early reader books have multiple lines on a page, introduce dialogue and more varied vocabulary, and may have sentences that carry across pages. Students typically learn through these books in late kindergarten through the beginning of second grade. *Llama, Llama Misses Mama* by Anne Dewdney is an example of a book at the beginning of this band. *Curious George* by Margaret Rey is the type of text that children can begin to read at the end of this band.

Transitional readers have solidified their skills to the point that they are able to read silently. They now have a large bank of high frequency words and continuously apply multiple reading strategies to solve problems while reading. They are learning to sustain reading over longer texts, including early chapter books. Students in this band, usually in second and third grades, enjoy reading books in a favored series. You can stretch these readers by encouraging them to read a variety of genres and informational texts. *A Kiss for Little Bear* by Elsa Holmelund Minarik is an example of a book at the beginning of this band. By the end of this band, readers have grown to read books like the *Magic Tree House* series.

Self-extending readers are reading orally with increasing fluency but often prefer to read silently. The books they read tend to be longer and require stamina to read over several days. They read fiction and nonfiction for enjoyment and to build background knowledge and apply this knowledge as they dig more deeply into books. As they read, students at this level draw upon multiple sources of information smoothly, analyze words in flexible

Figure 11.3 Matching Books to Readers

> ways, and continuously build higher level skills. This is an exciting stage of reading as children become absorbed in their reading, identifying with characters and making connections across texts that they have read. Typically, students begin to read these books in third grade. Often, more sophisticated picture books are categorized at this level; *Sylvester and the Magic Pebble* by William Steig is one example. *Ramona* books by Beverly Cleary are examples of chapter books at the beginning of this band and titles such as *Shiloh* by Phyllis Reynolds Naylor are at the end of this band.
>
> By fifth grade and into middle school, students should be entering the *advanced reader* stage. They read silently, effectively understand how words work and go beyond the text to interpret and deeply understand the texts they are reading. They can read for extended periods of time. Most exciting, they begin to read to better understand the world from philosophical, ethical and social perspectives. By middle school, readers begin to read much like adults do as they tackle increasingly complex texts. Books in this band include Roald Dahl's *Matilda* and Seymour Simon's *Galaxies* up to titles such as Lois Lowry's *The Giver* and J R R Tolkien's *The Hobbit*.

Figure 11.3 (Continued)

Support Staff

Tutors sometimes need to connect with the other support staff at the school, including special education teachers, counselors, and paraprofessionals. All of these people play critical roles in meeting the needs of diverse students. The teams offer specialized services, support individualized learning plans, and offer specific insights into students. Remember, it was additional support staff who told me that "Julio had beef with everyone," information that gave me a completely different perspective.

Strategies for Building a Strong Network of Support

Strategies for Effective Collaboration

Schools should set up parent–tutor communication portals. An online communication portal allows tutors and parents to share updates, resources, and feedback. The portal includes features for scheduling meetings (phone calls, emails, online discussion box), tracking student progress, and accessing educational materials. Tutors should communicate with parents often. Parents need to know what the plan is, how we are all working toward it, what each partner is doing, and how they can help. There should be a schedule set up for regular check-in times. Busy schedules can make it hard to get and stay in contact. It is crucial that tutoring programs offer flexible communication options, such as asynchronous messaging or virtual meetings, in order to accommodate different schedules. Regular communication between tutors and parents facilitates the exchange of important information about the student's progress, strengths, and areas needing improvement. This open dialogue allows for timely interventions and adjustments to the learning plan.

Share Resources and Strategies

Teachers and tutors can provide parents/guardians with the specific resources needed to support learning at home. This could be manipulatives, reference sheets, or a list of YouTube videos or digital games. It could also be targeted at visual flash cards or game boards. It could also include study guides, practice activities, and suggestions for creating a productive study environment at home. Teachers and tutors can also help parents learn about effective study habits, time management, and stress-reduction techniques.

Collaborative Goal Setting

Involving families and support staff in the goal-setting process ensures that everyone is aligned and working toward common objectives. Collaborative goal setting fosters a sense of shared responsibility and commitment to student success (see Figure 11.4). Everyone should be working together to set realistic, measurable, scaffolded goals with the student. This includes academic targets, behavioral objectives, and personal development goals. Clear goals provide direction and a shared purpose.

Challenges and Solutions

Language Differences

Tutors should have systems to communicate when there are language differences. Language differences can impede effective communication. Tutoring programs must plan for access to the information by providing translation services, bilingual staff, and

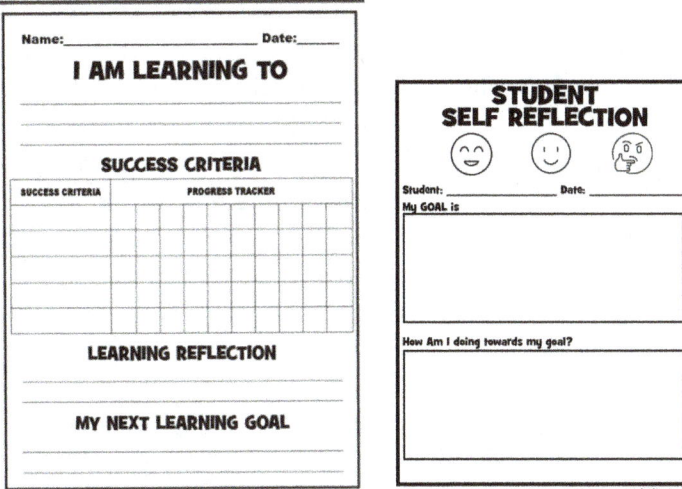

Figure 11.4 Student Self-Reflection Forms

multilingual resources. Schools must find ways to bridge the language differences and ensure that all families are included and feel comfortable coming and discussing their students.

Cultural Differences

Every student brings a wealth of cultural nuances and differences to the tutoring situation. Culturally relevant tutoring considers the different ways in which home help happens. Cultural misunderstandings can affect relationships between schools and families. Schools should prioritize cultural competence training for all staff, including their tutors, and adopt practices that respect and honor diverse cultural backgrounds.

Leverage Technology

Utilizing digital tools and platforms to facilitate communication, resource sharing, and collaborative planning can enhance connections within the support network. Doing it digitally also provides the advantage of a digital record. Schools should prioritize setting up a system in which communication between all the involved parties can occur digitally. It is very powerful to see the communication between the teachers, the tutors, and the families. We must always ask, "Is what we are doing helping the student?" "What specifically is helping?" "What could we be doing differently to improve achievement?" Digital platforms also provide a shared space in which to pass along resources so everyone can see the different ways we are approaching the situation. Also, putting up the progress monitoring allows information to be shared instantly with everyone, so the "What's next?" conversation can be had.

Summary

Building a strong network of support involving teachers, families, and support staff is fundamental to student success. By fostering effective communication, collaboration, and inclusivity, schools can create an environment in which all stakeholders work together to support the holistic development and academic achievement of students.

CHAPTER 12

High-Impact Tutoring and Multitiered Systems of Support

High-impact tutoring, especially when integrated into a multitiered system of support (MTSS), can move student achievement. High-impact tutoring can be a powerful tool in helping students who struggle unproductively in school, offering intensive, targeted instruction that complements the broader goals of MTSS. Districts that integrate MTSS and high-impact tutoring report that it "improves student outcomes, reduces implementation challenges, improves instructional coherence and streamlines operations" (National Student Support Accelerator & Blue Engine, n.d., para 2).

Understanding Multitiered Systems of Support (MTSS)

MTSS is a solution to improve educational outcomes for students. It builds upon and expands the scope of response-to-intervention (RTI) models. RTI focuses on improving academic outcomes through data-based decision-making, evidence-based instruction, and tiers of support. MTSS incorporates these elements of RTI but expands on them to proactively and responsively address social-emotional and behavioral needs as well as academic needs. Moreover, MTSS is a systemic solution that recognizes the importance of a curriculum that is grounded in high-quality instructional materials and culturally and linguistically responsive practices, teachers' need for ongoing professional learning, and collaboration between colleagues and between school, families, and community. Overseeing the successful implementation of the MTSS model, the administrative team at the school and district levels has an active role in establishing the vision for the work, establishing and monitoring the rollout of the program, and supporting shared leadership (American Institutes of Research, 2024; National Implementation Research Network, 2020). As noted in the research, "school principals played an essential role in implementing both during- and after-school tutoring programs. Education leaders served as gatekeepers of student and staff time, school space, and data/documentation on students' skills and instructional needs" (White et al., 2023).

The main systems components are:

1. Leadership: Leaders need to establish a clear vision for their program. This includes fostering a climate of ongoing learning for adults and a commitment to educational equity for the students. They need to articulate and communicate how the new approach (in this case, high-impact tutoring) fits within that vision. They also need to make sure that they allocate resources to support the vision—instructional materials, staff, scheduling, and finances.
2. Collaboration: People from different parts of the school need to work together. Instead of working in silos throughout the school, different departments come together to look at and provide the best education possible for the whole child.
3. Implementation sequence: "Successful implementation requires ongoing planning, continuous improvement, and

sustaining and expanding efforts." Teams must work together to assess, plan, create structures and processes, and address needs and review and evaluate how everything is working (American Institutes for Research, 2024).
4. Professional learning: The team must develop plans for professional learning based on the differentiated needs of the staff.

The main instructional components are:

1. Universal screening: All students are assessed to identify who may need extra academic and behavioral support.
2. A multilevel prevention and response system: This system allows different points of intervention that address the different needs of students by looking at Tier 1 instruction (the classroom curriculum) and how to integrate Tier 2 and Tier 3 instruction with Tier 1.
3. Data-based decision-making: Team works together to analyze and interpret the data and make decisions about instruction and intervention.
4. Progress monitoring: Ongoing use of assessments to determine where students are on the learning continuum and what comes next. The information helps to assess achievement, monitor, and evaluate success of the intervention and determine next steps (AIR, n.d., Essential components).

The MTSS components align well with high-impact tutoring. Universal screening can help to identify students who might benefit from it. Progress monitoring is an essential component of high-impact tutoring, helping to guide the tutor on what is working and what needs to be done next. With high-impact tutoring, there is a team approach to analyzing and interpreting the data and deciding next steps.

As the instructional leadership team meets to analyze school achievement toward goals and to determine next steps, they look at a variety of data points. Using the MTSS framework, they will identify areas for improvement and ways to support students through a tiered approach. The system is built on three (sometimes four) levels of instruction. **Tier 1** provides universal instruction and support for all students. Often, this is referred to as core instruction. **Tier 2** targets students who require supplemental help, while **Tier 3** offers more intensive, individualized interventions for students facing significant challenges. Some models include a **Tier 4**, which is for students who need even more specialized assistance, often in collaboration with outside professionals. Tiers increase the intensity of instruction. We can increase intensity by seeing students more often (days of the week), for more time, or both. We can also increase the intensity by decreasing the teacher-to-student ratio, allowing more individualized attention. It is helpful to think of these tiers as being layered. We have Tier 1, and then we layer more support on top of that as needed. The layers do *not* replace anything in the previous tier, though at the highest tiers, there may be some supplanting of instruction for the most complex students, which would be dictated by an individualized education program (IEP).

What the Experts Say

"High-Impact Tutoring is a critical layer of support, not a replacement for High-Quality Tier I instruction" (National Student Support Accelerator & Blue Engine, n.d., p. 12).

The goals of a multitiered system are prevention and early intervention, ensuring students don't fall too far behind. Continuous improvement efforts for the core curriculum and teacher professional knowledge are essential elements in improving student achievement. Schools also must identify students with learning gaps early on and begin providing layers of support immediately. But what about students who continue to unproductively struggle despite these efforts, particularly in the two foundational subjects of reading and math? This is where high-impact tutoring, a powerful Tier 2 and/or Tier 3 intervention, comes in.

Integration of High-Impact Tutoring Within MTSS

High-impact tutoring aligns beautifully with MTSS, particularly within Tiers 2 and 3. In an MTSS framework, high-impact tutoring provides targeted, intensive instruction to students who need more than what Tier 1 instruction can offer. If a student received a Tier 2 intervention in a small group, there may be data to support shifting to high-impact tutoring in order to make the gains necessary. High-impact tutoring typically involves frequent (often daily), one-on-one tutoring sessions, where students can receive personalized instruction that is tailored to their specific learning gaps based on data. Within MTSS, high-impact tutoring serves as a vital resource for students who are unproductively struggling. The beauty of high-impact tutoring is that it doesn't replace the core curriculum but enhances it, providing students with the scaffolding they need.

Schools can reduce implementation challenges by integrating high-impact tutoring with the core curriculum rather than doing it separately (NSSA, n.d.). Schools can increase instructional coherence by working with the same high-quality instructional materials used in Tier 1 instruction. If the school determines that it does not have a curriculum that meets the criteria for high-quality instructional materials, they may opt to use them for Tier 2 and Tier 3 instruction to provide immediate support for struggling learners while they invest in adopting other materials for the core curriculum. All of the intervention materials should be seeking to accelerate the instruction for students with unfinished learning. This means they are teaching the grade-level standards by "just-in-time" scaffolding. Integrating high-impact tutoring into the school's multitiered systems of support streamlines operations. It allows schools and districts to think about how they can use different funding sources such as Title I, IDA, and Title II (NSSA, n.d.).

Benefits of Incorporating High-Impact Tutoring Within MTSS

High-impact tutoring can be a game changer in reading and mathematics instruction, particularly for students who face persistent difficulties in learning. Within the MTSS framework, high-impact tutoring offers several clear benefits that make it a powerful intervention for enhancing educational outcomes.

Enhanced Responsiveness to Student Needs

One of the key benefits of high-impact tutoring is its ability to respond rapidly to student needs. In a typical classroom, a teacher may not have the time or specialized training to address every student's individual struggles, especially in subjects like reading and math, where students' challenges can vary widely. High-impact tutoring allows for targeted, individualized support in a one-on-one or small-group setting, providing focused attention where it's most needed. This heightened responsiveness ensures that students receive timely support, helping prevent learning gaps from widening over time, and ultimately closing those gaps.

Increased Access to Personalized Instruction

High-impact tutoring provides a level of personalization that is difficult or impossible to achieve in larger classroom settings. Sometimes, teachers don't have the content knowledge to help the students in their classroom. For example, many middle school teachers struggle with teaching nonreaders in middle school basic phonemic awareness because it is not something they have learned. In mathematics, where concepts often build on one another, a student's misunderstanding of foundational topics can make it challenging to grasp more advanced material. High-impact tutoring creates an environment in which instruction is tailored to the unique learning gaps of each student, offering the opportunity to revisit and reinforce specific skills. This is especially valuable for students at risk of falling behind, as the personalized nature of high-impact tutoring gives them the opportunity to work through challenging concepts at their own pace, under the guidance of a tutor.

Improved Academic Outcomes for Students at Risk

The results of high-impact tutoring speak for themselves. Research suggests that frequent, sustained tutoring can significantly boost academic outcomes for students who are at risk of failing or falling behind (Nickow et al., 2020). In mathematics, this often translates to more confidence, greater problem-solving abilities, and higher achievement in standardized tests and classroom performance. For students who have struggled in Tier 1 instruction, a high-impact tutoring framework offers a second chance—an opportunity to close the opportunity gap and gain the skills they need to succeed in school.

Strengthened Collaboration Among Educators and Stakeholders

High-impact tutoring also promotes collaboration. Tutors should work closely with classroom teachers, special educators, and other professionals to align their instruction with the broader goals of the student's learning plan. This coordination ensures that the interventions provided in high-impact tutoring are in sync with what's happening in the general classroom, creating a seamless support system. By fostering this collaboration, high-impact tutoring strengthens the overall educational ecosystem and helps everyone involved stay focused on the student's progress.

Challenges and Considerations

While the benefits of high-impact tutoring within MTSS are significant, there are also challenges and considerations to address to ensure its success.

Resource Allocation and Scalability of High-Impact Tutoring Within MTSS

One of the primary challenges is the resource-intensive nature of high-impact tutoring. Implementing the program requires a significant investment in both time and personnel. Finding qualified tutors, ensuring they are trained to deliver high-quality instruction, and scheduling regular sessions can be costly and complex (National Student Support Accelerator & Blue Engine, n.d.). Scaling high-impact tutoring across an entire school or district can be even more challenging, especially in communities with limited funding or access to educational resources. However, the long-term benefits for student achievement often outweigh the costs, particularly when the investment is made with clear goals and a strategic plan for resource allocation and implementation of high-impact tutoring.

Monitoring and Evaluating High-Impact Tutoring Effectiveness Within the MTSS Framework

Effectively integrating high-impact tutoring into the school program requires ongoing support, monitoring, and evaluation. Schools need systems in place to support the tutors, track student progress, assess the effectiveness of tutoring interventions, and make adjustments as necessary. This is not always easy to accomplish, particularly when multiple interventions are in place simultaneously. Regular data collection, collaborative reflection, and adjustment are critical to ensuring that high-impact tutoring remains effective and responsive to students' evolving needs. Schools must invest in the tools and ongoing professional development necessary to support this evaluation process.

Addressing Equity and Access Issues in High-Impact Tutoring Implementation

Another major consideration is ensuring equity in high-impact tutoring implementation. Students from underserved communities, particularly those from marginalized racial, socioeconomic, or linguistic backgrounds, often face the greatest barriers to academic success (Education Recovery Scorecard, 2024). It's essential that high-impact tutoring programs are designed with equity in mind, providing equal access to the high-quality support that students need. Schools must be mindful of the potential for inequities in high-impact tutoring availability, ensuring that all students—regardless of background—have access to the tutoring they need to thrive in the core subjects of reading and mathematics.

Strategies for Refining High-Impact Tutoring Implementation to Maximize Effectiveness Within MTSS

To maximize the effectiveness of high-impact tutoring, educators and school leaders must continually refine its implementation. This might include developing more flexible models that allow for a combination of in-person and online tutoring, enhancing tutor training to ensure consistent, high-quality instruction, and finding ways to engage parents and caregivers in the tutoring process. By staying flexible and responsive, schools can ensure that high-impact tutoring evolves to meet the needs of students while maintaining alignment with the MTSS framework.

Summary

Incorporating high-impact tutoring into an MTSS framework is a powerful way to support students who are unproductively struggling in reading and mathematics. The symbiotic relationship between high-impact tutoring and MTSS creates an environment in which students receive the individualized support they need while educators work together to ensure that no student falls through the cracks. Though challenges remain, the potential of high-impact tutoring to transform educational outcomes—particularly for at-risk students—is undeniable. With careful planning, consistent monitoring, and a commitment to equity, high-impact tutoring has the power to reshape the way we approach tutoring in the core subjects of reading and mathematics instruction in our schools.

Epilogue

Zach joined my fourth-grade class in late September. He transferred to our small independent school in the western US from a public school special education program. His parents were unhappy that he was not in a "least restrictive setting," which they felt would have been more appropriate for him. Zach had a lot of content knowledge, was very curious, and had strong social skills. He also had very significant reading delays. At the beginning of fourth grade, he had not yet grasped the alphabetic principles and basic phonics needed to decode primer-level books. Fortunately for Zach, his parents had the financial resources and tenacity to advocate for their child's education.

The task before Zach's team—his parents, the school administration, the school's learning specialist, and me as his classroom teacher—was to provide Zach with a strong curriculum program that would keep him engaged in learning and build his identity as a learner while also providing him with the highly structured instruction he needed in order to become a confident reader and writer. In the mid-1990s, this required us to imagine a new way of structuring a student's school experience. In planning his program, we knew that collectively, we had the knowledge and skills needed to design his learning.

We knew that we had to recognize the social, developmental, and academic needs of a nine-year-old boy. We needed to modify Zach's program in a way that kept him engaged in learning experiences with his neurotypical peers and that nurtured his dignity as a member of our learning community. We also needed to provide intensive instruction in basic phonics and the structure of the English language.

Zach participated in almost all aspects of our classroom studies. With the help of a teaching assistant (we were fortunate to hire an incredibly "cool" young man whom all the kids wanted to hang out with), Zach engaged in every aspect of our curriculum except Spanish. While his team valued the importance of learning a second language, we agreed that it was important to prioritize building his academics in English. The teaching assistant worked with Zach on his homework during Spanish blocks and supported him (and his classmates) with support in writing tasks. This freed Zach's after-school time for sports leagues and intensive Orton Gillingham tutoring. He received 90 minutes of tutoring four days a week after school. We used Books for the Blind and textbook resources to provide him with audio recordings of classroom texts (this was pre-Audible times!). His parents read his book club books to him at night so that he could participate in discussions.

Zach was highly aware of his challenges in literacy. Honest conversations with him about the purposes of this program were essential for his buy-in and the hard work that *he* needed to do. We also recognized that it was not lost on his classmates that Zach struggled with basic literacy tasks. We needed to be constantly aware of the impact of this on his self-esteem and identity as a learner. The TA's ability to support all students, our open appreciation of the knowledge and curiosity he brought to our community, a classroom culture that valued diversity and the need to differentiate instruction, and Zach's strong social and athletic skills helped to mediate some of those stressors.

Zach's determination to succeed with the program we had in place showed quick success. By October, this young man was able to read PD Eastman's classic *Are You My Mother?* (1960). We celebrated this achievement with him. We continued to support Zach in this program throughout the year. In winter, his book club was discussing *Maniac McGee* by Jerry Spinelli (1990). Zach's insights on character motivation were models for his club mates and prodded their ability to track character development and support their thinking with text evidence. In March, we had a huge breakthrough in class. Zach was reading *Mrs. Frisby and the Rats of NIMH* by Robert O'Brien (1971) with his book club. I remember that I was working with another group at a table nearby. The students in Zach's club decided to "popcorn read" a section of the text—a technique that has students volunteer to read aloud a small portion of the text to their classmates. From my vantage point, I heard Zach volunteer to read a paragraph aloud. My interest was piqued. When he finished, his group mates applauded him. I still get teary-eyed remembering this.

This story from my teaching took place in the early 1990s, before many of the initiatives that shape schooling today had been formalized. The formal structure of high-impact tutoring was in the future. Even so, we instinctively knew that students with unfinished learning can be successful in a program that makes sure students are active and valued members of their learning communities, when they receive data-based tutoring that is focused on unfinished learning and still connected to the classroom curriculum, and when the student is supported by a committed team. In this case, Zach had a strong team that included school administration, learning specialists, classroom teachers, and his parents. We used a detailed assessment of his learning profile—his academic skills, his social-emotional development and needs, and his interests and areas of expertise. As a team, we were committed to making sure he was integrated into the classroom culture and community and to developing strong, honest relationships with him so that we could openly address the challenges he was facing and to get his all-important buy-in.

This program did not have 100% of the criteria that research tells us are markers of a quality, effective high-impact tutoring program. Those criteria would be established in the future. This was probably also an ideal scenario that is not easily replicable in schools. However, this story demonstrates that schools and families working together creatively to address unfinished learning while also making sure that the student is a fully participating member of a classroom community can help the student make the progress needed to close achievement gaps.

References

Adams, A., Carnine, D., & Gersten, R. (1982). Instructional Strategies for Studying Content Area Texts in the Intermediate Grades. *Reading Research Quarterly*, 18(1), 27–55. https://doi.org/10.2307/747537

Almarode, J., Fisher, D., Frey, N., & Thunder, K. (2021). *The Success Criteria Playbook*. Thousand Oaks, CA: Corwin Press.

American Institutes for Research, AIR, Center on Multi-Tiered Systems of Support. (2024). *Welcome to the MTSS Center*. Retrieved from https://mtss4success.org/

AmeriCorps. (2021). *Leveraging National Service in Your Schools*. Retrieved from https://americorps.gov/sites/default/files/document/Leveraging-National-Service-in-Your-Schools.pdf

Armbruster, B., Lehr, F., & Osborn, J. (2000). *Put Reading First: The Research Building Blocks for Teaching Children to Read*. Washington, DC: The National Institute for Literacy. Retrieved from https://www.nichd.nih.gov/sites/default/files/publications/pubs/Documents/PRFbooklet.pdf

Austrew, A. (2022). *How to Prevent Your Kids from Losing What They Learned in School During Summer Vacation*. Retrieved November 23, 2024, from https://www.scholastic.com/parents/books-and-reading/raise-a-reader-blog/summer-slide.print.html

Balfanz, R., & Vaughn, B. (2020). *Connecting Social-Emotional Development, Academic Achievement, and On-track Outcomes*. The Everyone Graduates Center. John Hopkins University School of Education.

Bandura, A. (1977). Self-efficacy: Toward a Unifying Theory of Behavioral Change. *Psychological Review*, 84(2), 191–215.

Beck, I. L., McKeown, M. G., Kucan, L., McKeown, M. G., & Kucan, L. (2013). *Bringing Words to Life: Robust Vocabulary Instruction* (2nd ed.). The Guilford Press.

Beers, K. (2003). *When Kids Can't Read: What Teachers Can Do*. Portsmouth, NH: Heinemann.

Beers, K., & Probst, R. (2017). *Disrupting Thinking: Why How We Read Matters*. New York: Scholastic.

Belsha, K. (2024). *Many Schools Want to Keep Tutoring Going When Covid Money Is Gone. How Will They Pay for It?* Retrieved from https://www.chalkbeat.org/2024/02/01/how-schools-will-keep-tutoring-programs-after-esser-covid-funding-is-gone/

Birsh, J. R., & Carreker, S. (Eds.). (2018). *Multisensory Teaching of Basic Language Skills* (4th ed.). Paul H. Brookes Publishing Company.

Brophy, J. E. (1998). *Motivating Students to Learn.* Boston, MA: McGraw–Hill.

Center on the Developing Child, Harvard University. (2019). *What Is Executive Function? And How Does It Relate to Child Development?* Retrieved from https://developingchild.harvard.edu/resources/what-is-executive-function-and-how-does-it-relate-to-child-development/

Center on the Developing Child at Harvard University. (2014). *Enhancing and Practicing Executive Function Skills with Children from Infancy to Adolescence.* Retrieved from www.developingchild.harvard.edu

Center on Multi-Tiered System of Supports. (n.d.). *Student Progress Monitoring Tool for Data Collection and Graphing.* https://mtss4success.org/resource/student-progress-monitoring-tool-data-collection-and-graphing

Chall, J. (1983). *Stages of Reading Development.* New York: McGraw Hill Book Company as cited in Annenberg Learner. Retrieved from https://www.learner.org/wp-content/uploads/2019/06/RWD.DLU1_.ChallsStages.pdf

Chang, W. C., & Ku, Y. M. (2014). The Effects of Note-Taking Skills Instruction on Elementary Students' Reading. *The Journal of Educational Research*, 108(4), 278–291. https://doi.org/10.1080/00220671.2014.886175

Clay, M. (2017). *Concepts About Print, Second Edition: What Has a Child Learned About the Way We Print Language?* Portsmouth, NH: Heinemann.

Clements, D., & Sarama, J. (2024). *Learning and Teaching with Learning Trajectories.* Retrieved from https://www.learningtrajectories.org/

Clements, L. L., & Bernhard, J. Z. (2005). *A Problem-Solving Alternative to Using Key-Words.* 10(7), 360–365. Mathematics Teaching in the Middle School. NCTM.

Compton, D. L., Fuchs, D., Fuchs, L. S., Bouton, B., Gilbert, J. K., Barquero, L. A., Cho, E., & Crouch, R. C. (2010). Selecting At-Risk First-Grade Readers for Early Intervention: Eliminating False Positives and Exploring the Promise of a Two-Stage Gated Screening Process. *Journal of Educational Psychology*, 102(2), 327–340.

Connor, S., & Froehle, J. (2022). Approaching Observations as a Curious Colleague. *Educational Leadership*, 79(7), 50–55.

Darling-Hammond, L., Flook, L., Cook-Harvey, C., Barron, B., & Osher, D. (2020). Implications for Educational Practice of the Science of Learning and Development. *Applied Developmental Science*, 24(2), 97–140.

Davis, H. (2001). *Contemporary Educational Psychology 26*, 431–453. Retrieved from http://www.idealibrary.com

Dean, C. B., Hubbell, E. R., Pitler, H., & Stone, B. (2012). *Classroom Instruction That Works: Research-Based Strategies for Increasing Student Achievement* (2nd ed.). Alexandria: ASCD.

Dehaene, S. (2010). *Reading in the Brain: The New Science of How We Read*. New York: Penguin Random House.

Deepseek (2025). AI. Deepseek.com

Devine, T. G. (1987). *Teaching Study Skills: A Guide for Teachers*. Boston, MA: Allyn & Bacon.

District of Columbia: Office of the State Superintendent of Education. (2021). *High-Dosage Tutoring: A Proven Strategy to Accelerate Student Learning: Guide for Local Education Agencies*. Retrieved from https://osse.dc.gov/sites/default/files/dc/sites/osse/page_content/attachments/HighDosage-TutoringGuidance.pdf

Downey, J. A. (2008). Recommendations for Fostering Educational Resilience in the Classroom. *Preventing School Failure*, 53, 56–63.

Eastman, P. D. (1960). *Are You My Mother?* New York: Random House.

Education Recovery Scorecard. (2024). *Understanding the Post-COVID Education Recovery Gaps*. Retrieved from https://educationrecoveryscorecard.org/

Entress, C., & Wagner, A. (2014). Beyond "Hitting the Books": Teaching Science Students Strategies for Studying Independently. *The Science Teacher*, 81(4), 27–31. https://www.jstor.org/stable/43746928

Epstein, J. L., & Vorhis, F. L. (2002). Teachers Involve Parents in Schoolwork (TIPS) Processes. In Epstein, J. L., Sanders, M. G., Simon, B. S., Salinas, K. C., Jansorn, N. R., & Voorhis, F. L. (Eds.), *School, Family, and Community Partnerships: Your Handbook for Action* (2nd ed., pp. 291–324). Washington, DC: Office of Educational Research and Improvement (ED). Burbank, CA: Disney Learning Partnership. Pleasantville, NY: DeWitt Wallace/Reader's Digest Fund. Thousand Oaks, CA: Corwin Press.

Faulkner, V. N., & Cain, C. (2009). *The Components of Number Sense: An Instructional Model for Teachers. Teaching Exceptional Children*. Sage.

Fink, S., & Markholt, A. (2011). *Leading for Instructional Improvement: How Successful Leaders Develop Teaching and Learning Expertise*. San Francisco, CA: Jossey-Bass.

Finley, Todd Blake. (n.d.). *Feedback Strategies for Coaches and Administrators*. Retrieved November 11, 2024, from https://visiblybetter.cepr.harvard.edu/files/visibly-better/files/instructional-feedback-guidebook.pdf

Fisher, D., & Frey, N. (2017). Teaching Study Skills. *The Reading Teacher*, 71(3), 373–378.

Foorman, B., Beyler, N., Borradaile, K., Coyne, M., Denton, C. A., Dimino, J., Furgeson, J., Hayes, L., Henke, J., Justice, L., Keating, B., Lewis, W., Sattar, S., Streke, A., Wagner, R., & Wissel, S. (2016). *Foundational Skills to Support Reading for Understanding in Kindergarten Through 3rd Grade (NCEE 2016–4008)*. Washington, DC: National Center for Education Evaluation and Regional Assistance (NCEE), Institute of Education Sciences, U.S. Department of Education. Retrieved from the NCEE website http://whatworks.ed.gov

Frisby, B. N., & Martin, M. M. (2010). Instructor–Student and Student–Student Rapport in the Classroom. *Communication Education*, 59, 146–164. https://doi.org/10.1080/03634520903564362

Fryer, R. (2016). *The Production of Human Capital in Developed Countries: Evidence from 196 Randomized Field Experiments*. Cambridge, MA: National Bureau of Economic Research.

Frymier, A. B., & Houser, M. L. (2000). The Teacher-Student Relationship as an Interpersonal Relationship. *Communication Education*, 49, 207–219. https://doi.org/10.1080/03634520009379209

Gablinske, P. B. (2014). *A Case Study of Student and Teacher Relationships and the Effect on Student Learning*. Open Access Dissertations. Paper 266. Retrieved from https://digitalcommons.uri.edu/oa_diss/266

Gettinger, M., & Seibert, J. (2002). Contributions of Study Skills to Academic Competence. *School Psychology Review*, 31(3), 350–365.

Goethe, J. W. (1749–1832). Retrieved August 9, 2024, from https://www.gurteen.com/gurteen/gurteen.nsf/id/L004448/#:~:text=Quotations%20from%20Johann%20Wolfgang%20von,I%20help%20you%20become%20that

Goldsmith, M. (2003, Fall). Try Feedforward Instead of Feedback. *The Journal for Quality and Participation*, 26(3), 38–40.

Graham, S., & Hebert, M. (2010). *Writing to Read: Evidence for How Writing Can Improve. Carnegie Corporation Time to Act Report*. Washington, DC: Alliance for Excellent Education. Print.

Guryan, J., Ludwig, J., Bhatt, M., Cook, P., Davis, J., Dodge, K., Farkas, G., Fryer, R., Mayer, S., Pollack, H., & Steinberg, L. (2021). *Not Too Late: Improving Academic Outcomes Among Adolescents*. Cambridge, MA: National Bureau of Economic Research.

Guskey, T. R., & Link, L. (2022). What Teachers Really Want When It Comes to Feedback. *Educational Leadership*, 79(7), 42–48.

Hallinan, M. T. (2008). Teacher Influences on Students' Attachment to School. *Sociology of Education*, 81(3), 271–283. https://doi.org/10.1177/003804070808100303

Hamre, B. K., & Pianta, R. C. (2006). Student-Teacher Relationships. In G. G. Bear & K. M. Minke (Eds.), *Children's Needs III: Development, Prevention, and Intervention* (pp. 59–71). National Association of School Psychologists.

Hartl, S., & Riley, C. (2021). *High-Quality Curriculum Is a Transformation Tool for Equity*. Retrieved October 17, 2024, from https://ascd.org/el/articles/high-quality-curriculum-is-a-transformation-tool-for-equity

Hattie, J. (2009). *Hattie Ranking: 252 Influences and Effect Sizes Related to Student Achievement*. Retrieved August 10, 2024, from https://visible-learning.org/hattie-ranking-influences-effect-sizes-learning-achievement/

Hattie, J. (2018). *Hattie's 2018 Updated List of Factors Related to Student Achievement: 252 Influences and Effect Sizes (Cohen's d)*. Retrieved November 24, 2024, from https://visible-learning.org/hattie-ranking-influences-effect-sizes-learning-achievement/

Hayes Jacobs, H. (Personal Communication, 2005).

Henderson, A. T., & Mapp, K. L. (2002). *A New Wave of Evidence: The Impact of School, Family, and Community Connections on Student Achievement*. National Center for Family & Community Connections with Schools.

Hochman, J., & Wexler, N. (2024). *The Writing Revolution*. San Francisco: Jossey-Bass.

Hoover, J., & Patton, J. (1995). *Teaching Students with Learning Problems to Use Study Skills: A Teacher's Guide*. University of Virginia: Pro Ed.

Hoover-Dempsey, K. V., & Sandler, H. M. (1997). Why Do Parents Become Involved in Their Children's Education? *Review of Educational Research*, 67(1), 3–42.

Illustrative Mathematics. (2016). *Comparing Growth: Variation 1 and Comparing Growth: Variation 2*. Retrieved November 23, 2024, from https://tasks.illustrativemathematics.org/4

International Dyslexia Association. (n.d.). *Universal Screening: K-2 Reading*. Retrieved December 3, 2024, from https://dyslexiaida.org/universal-screening-k-2-reading/#:~:text=Research%20indicates%20that%20kindergarten%20screening,Jenkins%20&%20Johnson%2C%202008)

The IRIS Center. (2006). *RTI (Part 2): Assessment*. Retrieved from https://iris.peabody.vanderbilt.edu/module/rti02-assessment/

Janetos, H. (2024). *From Sound to Summary: Braiding the Reading Rope to Make Words Make Sense*. Independently Published.

Jenkins, J., Hudson, R., & Johnson, E. (2007). Screening for At-Risk Readers in a Response to Intervention Framework. *School Psychology Review*, 36, 582–599. https://www.academia.edu/27687650/Screening_for_At_Risk_Readers_in_a_Response_to_Intervention_Framework. https://doi.org/10.1080/02796015.2007.12087919

Kearns, D. M. (2016, August). *Student Progress Monitoring Tool for Data Collection and Graphing [Computer Software]*. Washington, DC: U.S. Department of Education, Office of Special Education Programs, National Center on Intensive Intervention.

Killian, S. P. (2021a). *8 Strategies Robert Marzano & John Hattie Agree on*. Retrieved November 24, 2024, from https://www.evidencebasedteaching.org.au/robert-marzano-vs-john-hattie/

Killian, S. P. (2021b). *What Everyone Needs to Know about High-Performance, Teacher Student Relationships*. Retrieved from https://www.evidencebasedteaching.org/crash-course-evidence-based-teaching/teacher-student-relationships/

Knowledge at Wharton Staff. (2006). *Is Your Team Too Big? Too Small? What's the Right Number?* Retrieved November 23, 2024, from https://knowledge.wharton.upenn.edu/podcast/knowledge-at-wharton-podcast/is-your-team-too-big-too-small-whats-the-right-number-2/

Li, X., Bergin, C., & Olsen, A. A. (2022). Positive Teacher-Student Relationships May Lead to Better Teaching. *Learning and Instruction*, 80, 101581.

Maiers, A. (2021). *12 Things Kids Want from Their Teachers.* Retrieved August 10, 2024, from https://angelamaiers.com/12-things-kids-want-from-their-teachers-2/

Making Math Moments (n.d.). The Progression of Proportional Reasoning From k-9: Make Math Moments Unit: The Foundation and Development of Multiplicative Thinking.

Marzano, R. (2012). Art & Science of Teaching/Teaching Self-Efficacy with Personal Projects. *Supporting Beginning Teachers*, 69(8), 86–87. http:www.ascd.org/publications/educational_leadership/may12/vol69/num08/Teaching_Self-Efficacy_with_Personal_Projects.aspxp

Marzano, R., & Pickering, D. (2005). *Building Academic Vocabulary, Teachers' Manual.* Alexandria, VA: ASCD.

Maxwell, J. C. (2002). *Teamwork Makes the Dream Work.* HarperCollins.

Moll, L., Amanti, C., Neff, D., & Gonzalez, N. (1992). Funds of Knowledge for Teaching: Using a Qualitative Approach to Connect Homes and Classrooms. *Theory into Practice*, 31(2), 132–141.

Mooney, M. (2018). *Why We Say "Opportunity Gap" Instead of "Achievement Gap."* Retrieved from https://www.teachforamerica.org/stories/we-say-opportunity-gap

Mosby, A., & Hamilton, S. (2022). *The Role of Cognition in the Gradual Release of Responsibility Model.* Retrieved from https://www.edutopia.org/article/role-cognition-gradual-release-responsibility-model/

Mosseson-Teig, C., & Cunningham, K. (2015). *Early Childhood Assessment in Mathematics Manual.* Retrieved from https://tnay.weebly.com/uploads/7/6/3/9/76395731/early_childhood_assessment.pdf

Muhammad, G. (2020). *Cultivating Genius*. New York: Scholastic.

National Association of School Psychologists. (2010). Self-Efficacy: Helping Children Believe They Can Succeed, 39(3). http:www.nasponline.org/publications/cq/index.aspx?vol=39&issue=3

National Implementation Research Network. (2020). *Implementation Stages Planning Tool*. Chapel Hill, NC: National Implementation Research Network, FPG Child Development Institute, University of North Carolina at Chapel Hill.

National Research Council. (2001). *Adding It Up: Helping Children Learn Mathematics*. Washington, DC: The National Academies Press. https://doi.org/10.17226/9822

National Student Support Accelerator. (2024). *Relationship-Building Activities*. Retrieved August 4, 2024, from https://studentsupportaccelerator.org/tutoring/instruction/relationship-building/relationship-building-activities

National Student Support Accelerator & Blue Engine. (n.d.). *High Impact Tutoring Playbook*. Retrieved November, 2023, from https://studentsupportaccelerator.org/sites/default/files/High_Impact_Tutoring_District_Playbook.pdf

Newton, R. 2016. *Math Running Records*. NY: Routledge.

Nicaise, M., & Gettinger, M. (1995). Fostering Reading Comprehension in College Students. *Reading Psychology*, 16, 283–337.

Nickow, A. J., Oreopoulos, P., & Quan, V. (2020). *The Impressive Effects of Tutoring on PreK-12 Learning: A Systematic Review and Meta-Analysis of the Experimental Evidence* (EdWorkingPaper: 20–267). Retrieved from Annenberg Institute at Brown University. https://doi.org/10.26300/eh0c-pc52

O'Brien, R. (1971). *Mrs. Frisby and the Rats of NIMH*. New York: Scholastic Books.

Owocki, G., & Goodman, Y. (2002). *Kidwatching: Documenting Children's Literacy Development*. ME: Heinemann.

Paper. (n.d.). *The Average Effect of Tutoring Programs on Academic Achievement*. Retrieved from https://pages.paper.co/high-dosage-tutoring

Papert, S. (n.d.). Hard Fun. *The Daily Papert*. Retrieved December 1, 2024, from https://dailypapert.com/hard-fun/

Piechurska-Kuciel, E. (2011). Perceived Teacher Support and Language Anxiety in Polish Secondary School EFL Learners. *Studies in Second Language Learning and Teaching*, 1, 83–100.

Pierson, R. (2013). Every Kid Needs a Champion. *Ted Talks*. Retrieved November 23, 2023, from https://www.ted.com/talks/rita_pierson_every_kid_needs_a_champion?subtitle=en

Pinkerton, P., Cortes, B., Dull, A., Fogarty, L., Whaley, H., & Nazario, L. (2017). *Teaching to Transform: An Instructional Practice Guide to Support Struggling Readers and Writers in Grades 6–12*. New York: NYC Department of Education.

Pintrich, P. R., & Schunk, D. H. (1996). *Motivation in Education: Theory, Research and Applications*. Englewood Cliffs, NJ: Prentice-Hall.

Reyes, R., Reyes, B., McIntosh, A., & Yang, D. C. (2010). Assessing Number Sense of Students in Australia, Sweden, Taiwan and the United States School Science and Mathematics. *School Science and Mathematics*, 99(2), 61–70. Retrieved January 15, 2024, from https://www.researchgate.net/figure/Six-Components-of-Number-Sense_tbl1_229794276

Robinson, C., Kraft, M., Loeb, S., & Schueler, B. (2021). *Design Principles for Accelerating Student Learning with High-Impact Tutoring*. EdResearch for Recovery. Brief #16. Retrieved from https://annenberg.brown.edu/sites/default/files/EdResearch_for_Recovery_Design_Principles_1.pdf

Robinson, C., Kraft, M., Loeb, S., & Schueler, B. (2024). *Design Principles for Accelerating Student Learning with High-Impact Tutoring*. Ed Research for Action. Brief #30. Retrieved November 10, 2024, https://studentsupportaccelerator.org/briefs/accelerating-student-learning-with-high-Impact-tutoring

Sawchuck, S. (2020). *High-Dosage Tutoring Is Effective, But Expensive. Ideas for Making It Work*. Retrieved August 4, 2024, from https://www.edweek.org/leadership/high-dosage-tutoring-is-effective-but-expensive-ideas-for-making-it-work/2020/08

Scarborough, H. S. (2001). Connecting Early Language and Literacy to Later Reading (Dis)abilities: Evidence, Theory, and Practice. In S. Neuman & D. Dickinson (Eds.), *Handbook for Research in Early Literacy* (pp. 97–110). New York: Guilford Press.

Shafer, L. (2016). *Summer Math Loss: Why Kids Lose Math Knowledge, and How Families Can Work to Counteract It*. Retrieved November 5, 2023, from https://www.gse.harvard.edu/ideas/usable-knowledge/16/06/summer-math-loss

Shahidi, F., Dowlatkhah, H. R., Avand, A., Musavi, S. R., Mohammadi, E. (2014). A Study on the Quality of Study Skills of

Newly-Admitted Students of Fasa University of Medical Sciences. *Journal of Advances in Medical Education & Professionalism*, 2(1), 45–50.

Shanahan, T. (2019). *How Important Is Reading Rate? Shanahan on Literacy.* Retrieved from https://www.shanahanonliteracy.com/blog/how-important-is-reading-rate#:~:text=Such%20rates%20have%20large%20standard,strategies%20with%20sufficiently%20challenging%20texts

Sparks, S. (2019). *Why Student Relationships Matter.* Retrieved April 10, 2024, from https://www.edweek.org/teaching-learning/why-teacher-student-relationships-matter/2019/03

Spinelli, J. (1990). *Maniac Magee.* New York: Little, Brown Books.

Thomas, P. (2020, March 1). *The Power of Relationship-Driven Tutoring.* Retrieved December 9, 2024, from Knack https://blog.joinknack.com/the-power-of-relationship-driven-tutoring

TNTP. (2018). *The Opportunity Myth.* Retrieved March 15, 2024, from https://opportunitymyth.tntp.org/

Treadway, L., Militello, M., & Simon, K. (2021). Making Classroom Observations Matter. *Educational Leadership*, 78(7), n.p. Retrieved November 10, 2024, from https://ascd.org/el/articles/making-classroom-observations-matter

Tutor.com. (2024). *High-Dosage Tutoring vs. High-Impact Tutoring: What's the Difference?* Retrieved November 23, 2024, from https://www.tutor.com/articles/high-dosage-high-impact-tutoring-analysis

Vaughn, S., Gersten, R., Dimino, J., Taylor, M. J., Newman-Gonchar, R., Krowka, S., Kieffer, M. J., McKeown, M., Reed, D., Sanchez, M., St. Martin, K., Wexler, J., Morgan, S., Yañez, A., & Jayanthi, M. (2022). *Providing Reading Interventions for Students in Grades 4–9 (WWC 2022007).* Washington, DC: National Center for Education Evaluation and Regional Assistance (NCEE), Institute of Education Sciences, U.S. Department of Education. Retrieved from https://whatworks.ed.gov/

Virginia Tech. (2011). Easy to Visualize Goal Is Powerful Motivator to Finish a Race or a Task. *ScienceDaily.* Retrieved March 15, 2023, from www.sciencedaily.com/releases/2011/08/110815143935.htm

Visible Learning. (n.d.). *Hattie Ranking: 252 Influences and Effect Sizes Related to Student Achievement.* Retrieved December 11, 2024, from https://visible-learning.org/hattie-ranking-influences-effect-sizes-learning-achievement/

Wechsler, N. (2024). The Writing Effect. *Minding the Gap*. Retrieved December 1, 2024, from https://nataliewexler.substack.com/p/the-writing-effect

White, S., Groom-Thomas, L., & Loeb, S. (2023). *A Systematic Review of Research on Tutoring Implementation: Considerations when Undertaking Complex Instructional Supports for Students* (EdWorkingPaper: 22–652). Retrieved from Annenberg Institute at Brown University: https://doi.org/10.26300/wztf-wj14

Wiggins, G. (2012). 7 Keys to Effective Feedback. *Educational Leadership*, 70(1), 10–16. Alexandria, VA: ASCD.

Wilmore, E. L. (2020). *High Impact Study Skills for Diverse PreK-12 Subgroups*. Eric-Education Resources Information Center.

Wolf, M. (2008). *Proust and the Squid: The Story and Science of the Reading Brain*. London: Icon Books.

Wolf, M. (2018). *Reader Come Home: The Reading Brain in a Digital World*. New York: Harper Collins.

World Bank Group. (2023). *Addressing Unfinished Learning: A Global Perspective*. Retrieved from https://www.worldbank.org/en/topic/education/publication/the-rapid-framework-and-a-guide-for-learning-recovery-and-acceleration

Yale, A. T. (2017). The Personal Tutor–Student Relationship: Student Expectations and Experiences of Personal Tutoring in Higher Education. *Journal of Further and Higher Education*, 43(4), 533–544. https://doi.org/10.1080/0309877X.2017.1377164

Yusefzadeh, H., Amirzadeh Iranagh, J., & Nabilou, B. (2019). The Effect of Study Preparation on Test Anxiety and Performance: A Quasi-Experimental Study. *Advances in Medical Education and Practice*, 245–251. https://doi.org/10.2147/AMEP.S192053. Retrieved December 1, 2024, from https://pmc.ncbi.nlm.nih.gov/articles/PMC6524999/#:~:text=Changing%20study%20habits%2C%20active%20learning,schedule%20can%20reduce%20test%20anxiety.&text=Students%20who%20suffer%20from%20test,problems%20in%20preparing%20for%20exams

Zollman, A. (2009). *Students Use Graphic Organizers to Improve Mathematical Problem-Solving Communications*. Middle School Journal. NMSA.org.

APPENDIX 1

Invitation-to-Participate Letter

Dear Families,

Our school is pleased to offer your child, _____, additional instruction in literacy/math. As we have discussed with you, your child would benefit from specialized support in this area to improve their academic skills.

This tutoring program will happen _____ times a week from _____ to _____. Your child will not miss any instruction or special programs that the rest of the class has at this time.

At the end of the first ten weeks of this program, we will provide you an update with how your child is progressing.

In order for your child to participate, we need your approval. Please sign and date at the bottom of this letter and return the tear-off portion to your child's teacher by next Friday, (date).

If you have any questions, please feel free to contact me.

Sincerely,

(insert coordinator's name here)
Tutoring program coordinator

****

I give permission for my child, _____, to participate in the tutoring program at school.

Signed: _____

Date: _____

APPENDIX 2

School Assessment Plan

Universal screeners are completed three times a year to track student achievement progress. If you use multiple screeners, you should answer this question for each screener system.

We use _____ for our universal screener. What information does it provide us about our learners?

Literacy Universal Screeners

This plan should ideally include foundational skills assessments, comprehension assessments, and writing assessments.

Grade	Beginning of Year	Mid-Year	End of Year
K			
1			
2			
3			
4			
5			
6			
*students with significant delays			

Math Universal Screeners

This plan should ideally include numeracy assessments, comprehension assessments, and writing assessments.

Grade	Beginning of Year	Mid-Year	End of Year
K			
1			
2			
3			
4			
5			
6			
*students with significant delays			

Diagnostic Screeners

Literacy: Diagnostic screeners should be given after students have been identified as needing additional support. These screeners should be aligned with the prior standards and provide information on how to target instruction to close learning gaps.

If you use multiple screeners, you should answer this question for each screener system.

We use _____ for our diagnostic screener. What information does it provide us about our learners?

Grade	Name of Screening System and What It Assesses
K	
1	
2	
3	
4	
5	

6	
*students with significant delays	

Diagnostic Screeners

Math: Diagnostic screeners should be given after students have been identified as needing additional support. These screeners should be aligned with the prior standards and provide information on how to target instruction to close learning gaps.

If you use multiple screeners, you should answer this question for each screener system.

We use _____ for our diagnostic screener. What information does it provide us about our learners?

Grade	Name of Screening System and What It Assesses
K	
1	
2	
3	
4	
5	
6	
*students with significant delays	

Progress Monitoring

How will we assess the progress our students are making as they participate in high-impact tutoring? Progress-monitoring tools should align with the instructional goals and the program being used to support student learning.

We use _____ for our diagnostic screener. What information does it provide us about our learners?

Grade	Name of Screening System and What It Assesses
K	
1	
2	
3	
4	
5	
6	
*students with significant delays	

Informal assessments take place ongoing and are used to modify groupings and instructional goals.

APPENDIX 3
High-Impact Tutoring Program Rubric

This program rubric is based on the Design Principles for Accelerating Student Learning by https://annenberg.brown.edu/sites/default/files/EdResearch_for_Recovery_Design_Principles_1.pdf

https://ssri.duke.edu/what-is-high-dosage-tutoring-and-why-does-the-states-investment-in-it-matter/

Design Principle	More Effective	Less Effective	Evidence in Our Program	Establishing Priorities for Next Steps
Frequency	3 or more sessions a week for 45 minutes for a minimum of 12–15 weeks	1–2 days a week 20–30 minutes a session Fewer than 10 weeks		
Group Size	Group size of 1 or 2 with like needs/learning profiles	Group size of 4 or more		

Tutors	Certified teachers or trained paraprofessional		Nonprofessional volunteers especially with limited training		
Focus	Priority standards. Research shows that a reading focus for K–2 and math focus for older students is shown to be most effective.		Classroom catch-up and homework help		
Measurement	Clear learning objectives with specific plans for using a variety of data to track student learning and ongoing informal assessments to inform instructional plans		Vague learning objectives Formal benchmark assessments only No diagnostic or progress monitoring		
Relationships	Consistent tutor who develops positive, caring relationships with students		Remote instruction or inconsistent tutor		
Curriculum	High-quality instructional materials linked to classroom learning		Homework help Remediation only with little connection to grade-level standards		

Scheduling	During the school day so that students are not missing the regular program	Before or after school or on the weekend; pull-outs where students miss classroom instruction or special classes
Delivery Mode	In person	Remote or asynchronous
Prioritization	Targeting students in a lower-performing grade level or focusing on literacy in lower grades and math in upper grades allows program to benefit from broader organizational commitment	Randomized groups
Initial Training & Ongoing Coaching	Preprogram and ongoing professional development	No training or preprogram training only

Appendix 3 | 145

APPENDIX 4
Observation and Feedback Template

Sample tool aligned to high-impact tutoring design principles (Robinson et al., 2024) to guide observations. Once you determine the focus criteria for observations that match your context, decide with your tutoring team what this might look like in classrooms. In order to prepare for "curious conversations," you can prepare sample guiding questions.

Principle	The vision of what that might look like in practice (examples)	Guiding questions to get the conversation started (examples)
Strong Positive Relationships With Students	Eye contact Friendly tone of voice Use of growth-mindset language Respect for home culture Consistent attendance and timeliness	I noticed that you . . . Can you talk about why you responded that way?

Use of Data	Student attendance trends Tutor takes anecdotal notes during session Tutor can explain how the notes/data help them understand the student better Uses assessment tools to track student progress	Looking at your notes and the data, what do you notice about student learning and/or student engagement? When looking at the data, what do you wonder about? How are you using your notes and the data to help you give corrective/actionable feedback to students?
Curriculum	Using the materials provided in the program Following lesson-plan template	Let's look at your lesson plans. Can you talk to me about how you go about making these planning decisions? How is the timing going? Do you find you have enough time for what you plan? Or not enough?
Training and Support	Participates in training and support provided	How is it going? What has been helpful in your training? What additional supports would you like?

For Product Safety Concerns and Information please contact our EU
representative GPSR@taylorandfrancis.com
Taylor & Francis Verlag GmbH, Kaufingerstraße 24, 80331 München, Germany

www.ingramcontent.com/pod-product-compliance
Lightning Source LLC
Chambersburg PA
CBHW051746230426
43670CB00012B/2186